WAR AND TERRORISM IN JEWISH LAW

Essays and Responsa

edited by

Walter Jacob

Solomon B. Freehof Institute for Progressive Jewish Law
Rodef Shalom Press
Pittsburgh, Pennsylvania

STUDIES IN PROGRESSIVE HALAKHAH
General Editor: Walter Jacob
Solomon B. Freehof Institute of Progressive Halakhah.
www.Jewish-Law-Institute.com

DYNAMIC JEWISH LAW
Progressive Halakhah - Essence and Application

RABBINIC – LAY RELATIONS IN JEWISH LAW

CONVERSION TO JUDAISM IN JEWISH LAW
Essays and Responsa

DEATH AND EUTHANASIA IN JEWISH LAW
Essays and Responsa

THE FETUS AND FERTILITY IN JEWISH LAW
Essays and Responsa

ISRAEL AND THE DIASPORA IN JEWISH LAW
Essays and Responsa

AGING AND THE AGED IN JEWISH LAW
Essays and Responsa

MARRIAGE AND ITS OBSTACLES IN JEWISH LAW
Essays and Responsa

CRIME AND PUNISHMENT IN JEWISH LAW
Essays and Responsa

GENDER ISSUES IN JEWISH LAW
Essays and Responsa

RE-EXAMINING JEWISH LAW
Essays and Responsa

THE ENVIRONMENT IN JEWISH LAW
Essays and Responsa

BEYOND THE LETTER OF THE LAW
Essays in Honor of Moshe Zemer

SEXUAL ISSUES IN JEWISH LAW
Essays and Responsa

POVERTY AND TZEDAKAH IN JEWISH LAW
Essays and Responsa

NAPOLEON'S INFLUENCE ON JEWISH LAW
The Sanhedrin of 1807 and its Modern Consequences

ONLY IN AMERICA
The Open Society and Jewish Law

WAR AND TERRORISM IN JEWISH LAW
Essays and Responsa

WAR AND TERRORISM IN JEWISH LAW

Essays and Responsa

edited by

Walter Jacob

Solomon B. Freehof Institute for Progressive Jewish Law
Rodef Shalom Press
Pittsburgh, Pennsylvania

CONTENTS

ACKNOWLEDGMENTS

The Freehof Institute of Progressive Halakhah again expresses its gratitude to the Rodef Shalom Congregation for its support in technical matters connected with this volume. Special thanks go to Hanna Gruen and Irene Jacob for their careful proof-reading of portions of this book.

PREFACE

War and warfare remain little explored regions of the halakhah. After defeat by the Romans in 70 C.E. Jews had no army nor were we permitted to serve in the armed forces of others till the Emancipation. There were no issues to debate. An occasional responsum dealt with peripheral issues. There was no sustained discussion. Most of the great codes of Jewish law do not even mention the topic.

Despite these realities or because of them, the topic needs to be discussed. The lands in which we live and the State of Israel are very much involved in warfare. Terrorism has become a major issue around the world. We may wish for a more peaceful and secure world, but must deal with the realities which face us.

The essays and responsa in this volume begin with a general overview of war as understood by Judaism, Christianity and Islam, the three major religions which concern us. This brief summary is intended to provide some background for the remainder of the book. As terrorism concerns us most, the book then continues with Mark Washovsky's essay on a halakhic view of the human rights and civil liberties issues which confront us as we deal with terrorists. He focuses on the balance which we try to maintain as we seek security.

Michael Stroh turns to suicide bombers and looks at them through the eyes of martyrdom and religious fanaticism. As western religions are so far removed from this phenomenon, it remains puzzling as well as frightening to us. Moshe Zemer's brief thoughts along with several thorough responsa view the hard choices to be made when dealing with the captives of terrorists. Families and governments are faced with this dilemma. Some additional topics akin to this theme were to be treated by two Israeli authors, but they were unable to produce those essays.

Pacifism may seem far removed from our realities, but precisely for that reason deserves a through examination which has been provided by Arnold Wolf ז"ל, who unfortunately died a year ago. A responsum looks at this possibility further

War and military service have become part of our lives, but for Judaism this is a new phenomenon. Emancipation and the manpower needs of modern armies meant that we were suddenly faced with military service in all the lands where Jews resided. We faced the obligation willingly, but with no doctrine of warfare in contrast to Christianity and Islam. The State of Israel had to face these issues while conducting a series of wars. These are the topic of two further essays.

The responsa published here deal with specific problems which needed answers from a Jewish perspective. As virtually nothing on this topic existed in the traditional literature, they reflect new beginnings. Several in this selection are taken from two small, collections of responsa issued during World War II in a joint effort of Reform, Conservative, and Orthodox authorities. They represent rare cooperation among the three American religious groups with their divergent approaches to the halakhah.

As with the previous eighteen volumes in this series, we invite further discussion through the medium of our journal, *HalakhaH*. We also hope to return to this topic with further research and analysis.

Walter Jacob
24 Kislev 5770

INTRODUCTION
Judaism, Christianity, and Islam on War

Walter Jacob

War and rumbles of war have been with us from forever. They are a constant companion to human existence and play an important role in the history of Judaism, Christianity, and Islam. In order to place this volume into a broader perspective, we will begin with a summary view of war in the three religions which concern us most.

JUDAISM ON WARFARE

For Jews this begins with the biblical period on. Yet, after the destruction of the ancient Jewish state until the establishment of modern Israel, Jews were rarely active participants in warfare, although we often suffered terribly from its consequences. World wide peace was the distant Messianic goal and only limited efforts were made to tame the horrors of war or to place it into a theological framework. Ecclesiastes took a practical rather than idealistic view of war when it stated there is "a time for war and a time for peace," placing peace second (Ecc 3:8).

Wars were dispassionately reported as a divine or political instrument in the Bible along with minimal practical legislation on combat. After that there has been little discussion until the modern State of Israel.

THE BIBLICAL BACKGROUND

The biblical past presents a record of endless wars and conflict;[1] it is the history of a small embattled nation, not too different from that of modern Israel, in more or less constant strife. We see this even in cursory reading of Joshua, Judges, I and II Samuel, I and II Kings, I and II Chronicles. God is sometimes depicted as a warrior as in the Song at the Sea (Ex 15.3) and as warlike (Ex 17:16, Jud 5:13; Ps 24.:8;). God also destroyed the instruments of war (Ps 76.4; Hos 1:7; 2:20) and brought an end to warfare (Is 2:4).

The limited biblical legislation governing combat was not discussed or expanded in the historical account or by the prophets. For example, there was no discussion of the idealistic legislation of Deuteronomy which permitted exemption from military service for those who had built a new house and not yet enjoyed it, planted a vineyard and not yet harvested it, become engaged, but were not yet married, and included anyone who was afraid (Deut 20:5 ff.). Before engaging the enemy, an opportunity to surrender had to be offered (Deut 20:10). There was a discussion of captives generally and of female captives whom a soldier wished to marry (Deut 21:10). A siege was not to destroy valuable trees (Deut 20:19 f.). War along with the treatment of the enemy was harsh, often cruel, and the reports contained only the facts without moral comment (Ex 17:9; Deut 7.16 ff.; 20:15 ff.; Josh 8:24 ff.; Josh 10.28 ff.; Jud 3:29; I Sam 27:9; I Sam 15:13 ff.; I Sam. 10:6 ff.; etc.). King Asa was reported to exclude any exemption from military service (I K 15:22) - the only biblical reference to the deuteronomic legislation. Mighty warriors were glorified at some length (I Chron 11:22 ff.) and detailed accounts of the army were given (I Chron 12:24 ff.; II Chron. 1:14 ff.). Warfare was taken for granted without comment (II Chron 13:2 ff.; 14:7; 17:12 ff.). Slaughter, taking of captives, and ransacking was simply recorded without comment (II Chron 28:6 ff). God was seen as a fighter (Ex 15:3 ff.), in Isaiah with its fierce imagery (Is 42:13 ff.;) and later (II Chron. 32:21). The historical records of the Books of Chronicles, present a theology which lauds warfare.

Military service was taken for granted and the horrors of war were described as a necessity of what we would euphemistically call "nation building." The ideal of a peaceful world was presented by the prophets as a distant dream of the Messianic Age (Jer 65:25; Micah 4:3; Is. 2:4); though they spoke out against all violence (Is. 60.18; Jer. 23.3; Ezek. 45.9). We should remember that prophets close to various kings, usually supported the war about to be fought (I K 22.6 ff, etc.) though not always as we hear from the prophet Jehu (I K 16.7). The biblical tradition did not preserve their messages. As the later rabbinic traditions rejected warfare in order to avoid the total destruction of the Jewish people, they suppressed the Books of Maccabees and kept them out of the canon. The popular holiday of Hannukah instead placed its emphasis on an insignificant miracle rather than political victory.

Rabbinic and Philosophical Discussions

The subsequent halakhic and philosophical literature made only the most limited effort to provide a theoretical framework for war. Talmudic scholars, far removed from the realities of war, did not elaborate on it. No tractate of the Talmud nor any major section of this vast work dealt with this topic or with the effect of war on non-combatants who have always been the main sufferers. The basis of all subsequent discussion is found in the Mishnah and Talmud (Sotah 44b) as well as parallel statements in the Sifre. The discussion there distinguished between "commanded wars" (*Milhemet mitzvah*) which are obligatory (*hovah*) and "permitted wars" (*milhemet reshut*) which are not obligatory. All of this really centered around the divine command to conquer the land of Israel which had been promised to Abraham and his descendants. Conquering the land of Israel was a commanded war and therefore obligatory while the wars of David and later kings which expanded the territory were not obligatory even though they dealt with lands which could be included in the vague original divine promise and its later interpretations.[2] A section in Talmud Hor 12 a and b further described the role of the high priest in making the declaration of Deut 20:3-5.[3]

The exemptions from military service mentioned in Deuteronomy were understood to apply only to the latter kind of warfare. A further discussion of "discretionary war" appeared in Sanhedrin (M. San 2:4; 20a) which demanded that such wars needed the permission of the Great Sanhedrin composed of seventy-one members or perhaps could be simply undertaken by the king. The matter became further complicated by the discussion in Sanhedrin 16a and Berakhot 3b which stated that the king must also seek the advice of the *urim vetumin* – in other words divine approval given through the priests. These conditions made a "discretionary war" not even theoretically possible.

Considering the bulk of the Talmud, the limited discussion on these few pages demonstrates the scant halakhic interest in war during these centuries. There was no desire to elaborate on the biblical texts or to develop a full theological approach to warfare and all the problems which it brought.

Maimonides (1135–1204) used these discussions as the basis for his chapters on warfare in his *Mishneh Torah* ("Kings and War" - *Hillkhot Melakhim* 5:1 ff). It is the only discussion of war in the halakhic literature till recent Israeli efforts. It mixes theoretical and very practical considerations. The other halakhic codifications such as the *Tur* and *Shulhan Arukh* did not include warfare along with all discussion of the ancient Temple worship as they were purely theoretical and these codifiers concentrated on the practical. As Maimonides is the primary source for all later writers, I will summarize the contents of these brief chapters.

Maimonides removed the problems facing a *milhemet mitzvah* or *milhemet hovah* by declaring that the king could declare it and expanding his interpretation of a "commanded war" to include both expansive efforts and those which are purely defensive. Later commentaries continue this discussion, agreeing or disagreeing - which echoes debates about the problems of contemporary Israel.

Maimonides discussed limitations placed upon the ruler in his conduct of war (Kings and Wars 5:1-6). He could initiate such a war if it was a "commanded war" (*milhemet mitzvah*) without the permission of a court and force his people to support it, expropriate property, build roads, etc. This was not the case with an optional war for which he needed the support of the Sanhedrin. A religious war (*milhemet hovah*) involved the destruction of the seven nations who opposed Israel's conquest (Deut 20:17) as well as their complete destruction; this included Amalek (Deut 25:19).

The next chapter (Kings and War 6) stated that a king could engage in an optional war only after making a peace offer to his opponent. If the terms were accepted and the people followed the seven Noahide commandments, paid tribute and accepted other conditions - some quite harsh, they would not be slain. These conditions did not apply to the conquest of the land of Israel, nor to Moab and Ammon.

When a city was besieged, the opportunity for flight had to be left (Nu 31:7) by surrounding it on only three of its four sides. The biblical injunction against cutting down fruit trees was to be observed and the water source also should not be damaged. All unnecessary destruction of personal property, clothing or food was to be punished by the court.

The Jewish army could lay a siege three days before *shabbat* and could continue to fight even on *shabbat*. Those who fell in battle were to be buried on that spot. The soldiers in a military camp were permitted dubious food and were exempt from various ritual and *shabbat* regulations. The sanitation of the camp was to be observed (Deut 23:13 f.).

The role of the priest and the conditions of military service were also discussed (Kings and Wars Chapter 7), so that those who were excused (Deut 20:5-7) could leave. Afterwards the priest encouraged soldiers to fight well (Deut 20:3 ff.) or be dismissed so as not to affect their comrades. The legislation of those excused was expanded beyond the biblical statements to include talmudic discussions, so for instance, any kind of house, even a new barn exempted a soldier. On the other hand "faint hearted" was interpreted as physically unfit. These conditions only applied to "permissive wars" not to the conquest of the Land of Israel or defensive wars which were obligatory upon everyone. Fleeing soldiers were to have their legs broken.

In the last chapter of this section (Kings and Wars 8) Maimonides discussed conditions prevailing after victory. He permitted prohibited food including pork and wine. A soldier who engaged in sex with a captured woman was excused; it was understood as a concession to the evil impulse (*yetzer hara*). If he wished to marry her, she must convert without coercion and he had to wait three months before marrying her (Deut 21:11-12). If she did not convert, he had to free her.

The final chapters of this section (Kings ans Wars 11 and 12) dealt with the Messianic Age of permanent peace. Maimonides did not deal with war in his philosophical work, *Moreh Nivukhim* (*Guide to the Perplexed*). When we look to Jewish philosophical writings from Philo (ca. 40) through Saadiah (882 – 942) to the twentieth century, we find nothing except the most incidental discussions of warfare.

There was no effort by any Jewish thinker to tame the effects of warfare or to place realistic restrictions on the warring parties. As Jews had no army or tradition of fighting and were not involved in military service or a party to such conflicts except incidentally, no theories developed. Even in periods of Jewish history when there was more contact with the surrounding intellectual world, the discussions of Christian and Islamic thinkers on warfare were not noticed by Jewish scholars. Wherever Jews lived, they prayed for their rulers and in times of war for the success of their armies. In modern times such prayers are found in all prayer books. Nowadays they often also include Israel and the Israeli conflicts.

Throughout this long history, no theories of pacifism were created.[4] Although peace remains an ideal and continues to be mentioned often in public and private prayer as well as sermons. No theological, philosophical, or halakhic basis for pacifism developed. Within the Reform movements of the last two centuries some vague stirrings toward pacifism emerged but never with much of a following.

In the contemporary world efforts to create a Jewish system of military ethics continue to be made. Most try to base themselves on Maimonides as well as the various talmudic statements which dealt with self defense and the duty to save the life of one's neighbor. Those statements, however reflect non-military situations.[5]

As we approach this topic within this volume, we will see that warfare has remained on the periphery of Jewish religious discussion until the creation of the State of Israel. There the focus has been narrow and dealt with specific situations. There is no "just war" theory. As warfare affects Jews in the Diaspora and Israel we cannot avoid coming to terms with it or engaging in discussions with non-Jewish thinkers who have tried to work out a series of approaches through the centuries.

CHRISTIANITY ON WARFARE

As we view the issues of war in the context of two major world religions, the limits of Jewish discussions become even clearer. Islam and Christianity have spent considerable thought on the underlying questions as have other religions with which we have less contact.

The New Testament has some powerful statements which would oppose war. "All that take the sword shall perish with the sword " (Mt 26:52), "love your enemy" (Luke 6:28, 35). On the other hand military symbolism is used frequently "Do not think that I have come to bring peace to the world; no, I did not come to bring peace, but a sword" (Matt. 10:34). "He does not bear the sword in vain, for he is God's minister." (Rm 13:4) and military imagery "No man being a soldier of God, entangles himself in secular business" (2 Tim. 2:4).

Church Fathers

As early Christianity developed it had eschatological hopes and rejected any participation in war. The military imagery used by early Christians was understood as referring to the eschatalogical battles of the end of the world or inner battles of faith within an individual. Martyrdom found a foundation in the tale of the widow and her children of II Maccabees,[6] so the war filled Books of the Maccabees were included in the canon. The Church Fathers, Tertullian and Origen opposed any participation in military forces. However, this changed after Christianity became the official religion of the Roman empire. The great Christian philosopher, Augustine (354–430), who based himself on Aristotle, could state "we make war so that we may live in peace."[7] in his *City of God* , Augustine saw war as necessary to defend the "heavenly city." This was a "Just War." Furthermore wars were inevitable in the "earthly city" due to human failings. Just wars would eventually move humanity toward its peaceful destiny. Augustine and Ambrose of Milan (339–397) also called for military force against heretics.[8]

Middle Ages and Renaissance

Efforts to halt irregular warfare which sprang up constantly led to the "Peace of God" introduced by bishop Guy of Anjou in 975 at the Council of Le Puy; it intended to help the peasantry and the Church. Another such effort called the "Truce of God" prohibited fighting on certain days and seasons, but this was never very successful.

The Christian theological position toward warfare became clearer through the systematic work of the Italian canon scholar,

Gratian in his *Decretum* (1140), a work which became basic to canon law. Through it the "Just War Theory" became understood as primarily based upon revealed law.[9] His work listed protected classes of people which later included all non-combatants within Christendom except Jews and heretics.

Thomas Aquinas (1225–1274) considered wars justified when declared by the proper authority, when the cause was just, and when they advance the good   Wars which could be designated as holy became part of Christianity; the authority to declare such a war was vested in rulers and the pope.   So Urban II proclaimed the First Crusade in 1095, as a holy war to defend the Church against Islam. Clergy were authorized to accompany the troops.

REFORMATION AND MODERN TIMES

The Reformation and the wars which it brought led to further definitions of "Just Wars" among Protestant thinkers, so Martin Luther (1483 – 1546) acknowledged the "Just War" theory as did John Calvin (1509 – 1564); both defended the rulers who acted upon it; the profession of soldier was considered legitimate despite all the bloodshed that it brought.[10]

The inhuman Spanish policies toward the American Indians aroused considerable anger and led to the idea of placing moral limits on warfare. This was worked out in a major way by Francisco de Vitoria (1483–1546). His writings and those of contemporaries led to efforts to limit the cruelties of warfare and conquest. In Holland Hugo Grotius (1583 –1645) went further and rejected religious reasons for warfare and placed war into the context of natural law. He divided natural law into those which expressed the will of God and those which are the product of human reason. War may be a "necessary evil," but it had to be regulated. Moral laws applied to the state as well as individuals. Rational rather than religious impulses were to be determinative.   Furthermore by emphasizing rules of warfare, a tradition of civilizing warfare began.[11] The enormous loss of life and destruction caused by the Thirty Year War encouraged this new line of reasoning. These thoughts were further developed by John Locke (1632 – 1704).   As he lived through England's civil war, he understood war as part of the "fundamental law of Nature."   That, however, could be overcome by civil society and the civil contract through which government is created. This then defined the right to wage war.

In the more recent centuries although the "Just War" theories survive, more emphasis has been placed on rejecting war entirely. Reinhold Niebuhr (1892–1971), however opposed this as too idealistic as it meant shirking one's role in society and so supported World War II.[12] Pope Pious XII and Paul VI rejected aggressive war while John XXIII was a pacifist.

ISLAM ON WARFARE

Islam, from its very inception considered war as an instrument of its holy mission to convert all unbelievers. This is one of the meanings of the term *jihad*, which also includes the struggle for faith, good works, and proper speech. Mohamed participated in such wars with the unbelievers as recorded in the Qur'an (2:190-93; 4:91-93; 8:39-40; 9:13, 29 etc.) This warfare (*dar al-harb*) is obligatory and its goal is universal peace when Islam has prevailed religiously and politically. This became the ideal of Sunni Islam. While Shi'ite traditions limit *jihad* to defensive measures until the return of the hidden Imam. During such warfare, the fate of conquered people was clearly spelled out as for example by Abu Yusuf (798). Their lands and possession now belonged to the conqueror and they had a choice between conversion and death.[13] Ibn Abi Zayd al-Qayrawani (996) went into additional detail as did others later.

MIDDLE AGES

The great philosopher, Averroes (1198) dealt with the legal obligation to participate in a war, the damage which may be afflicted on an enemy, and the possibility of a truce. He also discussed the aims of warfare and provided a masterful summary of legal obligations. Further details have been added through the centuries, so Ibn Taymiyya, whose writings are both general and legal dealt with specific situations.[14] Al-Hilli (1277) dealt in great detail with the nature of tribute which may be imposed and the type of behavior expected from conquered subjects as well as the reasons for permitting a truce.[15]

The decision to wage war originally rested in the hands of the direct descendants of Muhammed.   This worked until a rupture occured after the murder of the third Caliph, 'Ali.   The Battle of Karbala brought a final rupture with the Sunni following the caliph and the Shi'a waiting for the return of the hidden Imam.   For the Sunnis religious and political authority are united; for Shi'ites it is divided; religious authority lies with the imam and only defensive *jihad* is possible.[16]

Originally decisions made about war and conquest were intended primarily to deal with polytheists; when many lands with monotheistic religions were rapidly conquered, concessions were made to people of the book, i.e. Jews, Christians, and Zoroastrians.   Their followers were understood as monotheists of a less desirable form which could be tolerated in an otherwise all Islamic society. This also proved a useful way of integrating and using the skills of these minority groups, a necessity as the conquerors had not been prepared for the rapid conquest of so many lands.   Such believers were relegated to second class citizenship and remitted a tributary tax for the privilege of existing under Islamic sovereignty.

Jihad carried missionary fervor from the Arabian desert into Asia and to the boundaries of Europe.   It led to a millennia of bitter conflict in which Jews were generally bi-standers, suffered the outrages of war, and were then given subsidiary status in peace time. When the passions of *jihad* were exhausted, better conditions could emerge as in the Golden Age in Spain (1280–1340) and occasionally later.   Within this framework war was, nevertheless, understood as basically evil.   It was tolerated only in the service of bringing people to Islam.   Holy war was one of the acts of piety enjoined upon Muslims; it followed faith, prayer, fasting, and pilgrimage, all essential acts of piety. War was permitted to be destructive force which included laying waste date palm groves, vineyards, etc.[17]

War as a holy enterprise whose goal was peace was justified by virtually all the great Islamic theologians, both Sunni and Shi'ite.   As Islam is a judicial system different theories lead to different practical details.   Religious and political leadership were theoretically united, however, practical adjustments were made throughout the centuries. The tensions created through differing decisions by various leaders played an important role as most recently in the Iran vs. Iraq war as well as wars with the secular states of the West. The fervor of *jihad* has diminished in those Muslim countries which have become secularized.

The philosophical and theological approaches to warfare continue to be developed within various religious groups and sub-groups. Many Islamic leaders emphasize peaceful paths of bringing the world to Islam. A missionary zeal remains powerful among its followers. For some warfare remains very much on the Islamic agenda. On the other hand statements as the Cairo Declaration of Human Rights (1990) demonstrate some moderation, but only within the limits of Shariah.

I hope that the brief summaries provided in this introduction will place the place the essays in this volume into a broader context and lead to better understanding.

Notes

1. The German biblical scholar von Rad tried to organize the very different accounts into a system which is interesting, but problematic. D. Gerhard von Rad, *Der Heilige Krieg im alten Israel*, Goettingen, 1958.

2. Even a brief review of the boundaries presented in the various biblical books reveals enormous discrepancies. During my studies for the rabbinate at the Hebrew Union College I was almost tempted by a prize essay which demanded that these boundaries be investigated. A brief exploratory view of the topic revealed its complexity and I did not proceed further.

3. The following matters were found in other sections. Female prisoners could be married after following the biblical prescriptions (Jeb 48b). The prisoners of war became slaves (Git 38a). Booty taken (San 20b) was divided between the ruler and the soldiers. Soldiers were permitted to eat food found in the enemy's possession, even if it was normally ritually forbidden (Hul 17a).

4. Although there have been sermons on the subject; they dealt with a very specific conflict and did not attempt to formulate a broad Jewish approach to pacifism.

5. Nahum Rakover, _Otzar Hamishpat_, Jerusalem, Part 1, 1970, Part 2, 1990 for a detailed bibliography. _Tehumin_ Vol. 4, 1983); Vol. 8 1988 with a series of essays; J. David Bleich, "Preemptive War in Jewish Tradition," _Contemporary Halakhic Problems_ III, New York, 1989, "Nuclear Wafare," _Tradition_, Vol. 21:84 ff.; "Intafada and the Gulf War," _Contemporary Halakhic Problems_ IV, 351 ff pp. 251 ff. Gerald Blidstein, "The Treatment of Hostile Civilian Populations," _Israel Studies_ Vol. 1:2, 1996, pp. 27 ff.; Michael J. Broyde, "Military Ethics in Jewish Law," _Jewish Law Association Studies XIV_ (ed. Elliot Dorff), London, 2007, pp. 1, ff.; Shlomo Goren, "Combat Morality and Halacha," _Crossroads_, 1987, Vol. 1:211 ff. 1987; _Meshiv Milkhamah_, Jerusalem, 1983-1994, 4 vols.

6. II Macc. 6:9 ff; Eleazar 6:18-31; Seven brothers and their mother 7:1-40.

7. Aristotle, _Politics_.

8. Ambrose, _On the Christian Faith,_ 2.14. 136-143; Augustine, _Contra Faustum_ 22.74-75.

9. Davis Brown, _The Sword, the Cross, and the Eagle_, New York, 2008.

10. Martin Luther, _Temporal Authority: To What Extent It Should be Obeyed,_ 1523.

11. Hugo Grotius, _On the Law of War and Peace_, 1625.

12. Reinhold Niebuhr, "Must We Do Nothing?" _War in the Twentieth Century_, ed. Richard B. Miller, Louisville, 1992.

13. Abu Yusuf, _"Kitab al Kharaj,"_ The Legacy of Jihad, (ed. A. G. Bostom), Amherst, 2005, pp. 174 ff.

14. Ibid., 165 ff. Averroes, _"Bidayat al-Mudjtihid;"_ Ibn Taymiyya, _"Al-Ssyasa ak-Shariyya,"_ The Legacy of Jiyad, pp. 147 ff.

15. Al-Hilli, _"Shara'I'U 'L-Islam,"_ The Legacy of Jihad, pp 205 ff.

16. Majid Khadduri, "The Law of War: _The Legacy of Jihad_," (ed. E. G. Boston, pp. 305).

17. Ibid., p. 90.

TORTURE, TERRORISM, AND THE HALAKHAH
Jewish Law and the Elusive Balance Between Public Security and Human Rights

Mark Washofsky

Terrorism, defined as "premeditated, politically motivated violence perpetrated against noncombatant targets by subnational groups or clandestine agents,"[1] threatens the lives and safety of the people of all nations. In this paper, however, I want to focus upon the danger that terrorism poses to the nation as a state, an organized politico-legal structure. In particular, I am concerned with the nature of the response to terrorism adopted by democratic states such as the ones in which we live. Fundamental to our Western notion of liberal democracy is the principle of the rule of law,[2] which places clear and substantive limits upon the power of the state to enforce its will upon its citizens.[3] In particular, as a leading contemporary legal philosopher notes, "Law insists that force not be used or withheld, no matter how useful that would be to ends in view, no matter how beneficial or noble these ends, except as licensed or required by individual rights and responsibilities flowing from past political decisions about when collective force is justified."[4] Our societies accordingly cast a suspicious eye upon proposed policies that, while advertised as essential to safeguard public security, would result in increasing governmental intrusion upon the private realm. At the same time, the maintenance of public security is arguably the first and most basic responsibility of any government. The increasing frequency of terrorist actions against civilian populations has led many citizens of Western nations to demand the imposition of tough security measures that violate the liberties and civil protections that the law has traditionally guaranteed to the individual. The "danger" of which I speak, therefore, is twofold. On the one hand, the government's response to terrorism, if it is too forceful, can endanger the rule-of-law values that are an intrinsic element of our Western notions of democracy. Yet if that response is not forceful enough, the people may lose confidence in the government's power to protect them and replace it with a regime that promises security at the cost of the further suppression of individual freedoms. The question, then, is where to draw the line between public security and the rights of the individual, to achieve both these essential ends of government without sacrificing the one to the other. The search for this balance has become one of the most urgent tasks in contemporary law and politics.

At first glance, the *halakhah* would seem to offer little usable guidance on this subject. We are speaking, after all, of how modern, secular states might respond to the challenge of terrorism, and the *halakhah*, rooted as it is in ancient and medieval religious texts, is neither modern nor secular. It is well known, moreover, that individual "rights" and "liberties" are concepts foreign to the Jewish legal tradition, which tends instead to speak of the duties and obligations that the individual owes to God and Torah.[5] To the extent that the major halakhic compendia speak directly to the issue of national emergency, they grant extraordinary, virtually unlimited powers to the governmental authorities.[6] This surely does not aid us in the quest for "balance" between the conflicting requirements of individual freedom and national security. Still, the inquiry is a vital one that deserves our careful attention, for the following reasons:

1. Given that Judaism is a religious tradition that expresses itself largely through practice and observance, *halakhah* is absolutely central to any understanding of the Jewish experience. The intellectual and rhetorical discourse by which Jews have historically arrived at their understandings of correct practice – the answer to the question "what does Torah/God require that we do?" – is the language of Jewish law, crystallized in the halakhic literature. If, therefore, Jewish tradition offers teaching, guidance, and direction on issues of *political* practice, we are likely to discover that instruction by studying the halakhic sources. To put this another way, any authentic *Jewish* approach to questions of torture and terrorism, to the conflict between personal liberty and communal security, must be rooted in the halakhic literature and tradition.[7]

2. The fact that Jewish law speaks in terms of "duties" rather than of "rights" does not mean that the latter concept is entirely foreign to halakhic analysis. The existence of a legal duty can be said to establish a corresponding expectation (= "right") by others that the duty will be performed. For example, the obligation imposed upon a court to "do justice," to conduct its inquiry in accordance with clear rules of evidence and procedure, is tantamount to a "right" to due process of law. Similarly, although Jewish law does not know of a formal "right to privacy," it does define excessive prying into the domain of another person as a tort (*hezek re'iyah*, literally "damage caused

by seeing"), and it prohibits persons from engaging in verbal activity that damages the reputation of others (*lashon hara*; *rekhilut*; *hamotzi shem ra*), even though the latter may not be actionable in court.[8] From such details it would be possible to derive the existence of what, in practical terms, would amount to a right to privacy, a reasonable expectation that others will leave one alone in one's own domain or personal sphere of activity.[9] It is therefore appropriate to speak of civil and political "rights" in the *halakhah*, so long as we understand them as obligations to respect and to protect the vital interests of each individual.

3. Finally, this task is of special urgency to us as liberal Jews, particularly to those of us engaged in the study and development of liberal *halakhah*. Our task is to demonstrate in fact what we know to be true: that Jewish law is at bottom progressive and dynamic, "ethical in its very essence,"[10] a discourse that possesses sufficient resources to speak to every issue of religious practice in a sufficient and satisfying way. We are committed to the proposition that Jewish law *does* provide guidance on matters such as this and that this guidance can reflect the liberal and progressive values that characterize our vision of Judaism.[11]

What remains is to act on that commitment. The goal is to formulate an understanding of our ethical responsibilities to our nation and to the world community under the very difficult challenges posed by the growth of international terrorism. How does Jewish law, *as we understand it*, teach us to balance the conflicting demands of liberty and security? I don't pretend to offer here a systematic answer to that question. Much work, involving a thorough and precise study of the sources, remains to be done. This essay is intended rather as a decidedly preliminary sketch of one of the major issues.

That issue is torture, one of the most pressing and perplexing difficulties raised by the conflict I refer to here. It may happen -- how frequently is difficult to say, since governments understandably do not keep good records on this -- that security forces will arrest a person who may possess information deemed vital to public safety. Perhaps he is a member of a terrorist group; perhaps he has come into contact with the members of such a group. The police want the information that he has or might have, but the only way to induce him to reveal that information is through the use of torture. That word, I stress at the outset, is by no means easy to define. As one scholar notes, although "torture" has been widely discussed in legal literature, these debates have not settled on a uniform definition, and many lawyers and judges have used the term *without* defining it.[12] It is clear, of course, that "torture" involves a measure of physical abuse. Modern Hebrew, which includes the writings of jurists and political theorists, translates the word as `*inu'i*, drawn from a Biblical Hebrew root that evokes the sense of physical affliction or suffering, whether imposed by an oppressor (*e.g.*, Exodus 1:11-12, Deuteronomy 26:6) or undertaken by an individual for religious reasons as act of contrition or self-denial (*e.g.*, Leviticus 16:29 and 31). But how *much* abuse is required in order for an action to qualify as "torture"? Most interrogation of criminal suspects takes place under conditions that cannot be described as pleasant, but we presumably do not consider interrogation on a prima facie level to be identical with torture. Moreover, investigators can employ any number of non-physical techniques, ranging from the making of threats against family members to the ceaseless playing of loud music, that easily fall under the category of mental or psychological abuse; are these to be considered torture? One international compact includes the infliction of non-physical suffering in its definition:[13]

> (t)he term "torture" means any act by which severe pain or suffering, whether physical or mental, is intentionally inflicted on a person for such purposes as obtaining from him or a third person information or a confession, punishing him for an act he or a third person has committed or is suspected of having committed, or intimidating or coercing him or a third person, or for any reason based on discrimination of any kind, when such pain or suffering is inflicted by or at the instigation of or with the consent or acquiescence of a public official or other person acting in an official capacity. It does not include pain or suffering arising only from, inherent in or incidental to lawful sanctions.

Notice, in addition, that the above standard makes no effort to specify the intensity of inflicted suffering, whether physical or mental, necessary to qualify an act as torture. The critical aspect is the *intent* of the measures undertaken by law-enforcement officials. On the other hand, the title of another compact suggests that "torture" is substantively distinct from "cruel, inhuman, or degrading" treatment, though it, too, does not attempt to offer a precise definition of its terms. This has led observers to conclude that the document should be read as "a living text, to be interpreted within the understandings current" in the societies that live by it.[14] This is a reasonable observation, one that reflects both the uncertainties surrounding our definitions as well as the moral urgency we ascribe to them. We may disagree among ourselves as to precisely which acts qualify as torture; at the same time, we know that there *is* such a thing as torture and that we must respond to it as a legal and moral issue.

For the purposes of this paper, perhaps the best I can do is to adopt the old "I can't define it but I know it when I see it" definition: "torture" is anything that would strike the reasonable observer as such. This, in fact, is the standard adopted by the United States Supreme Court in a landmark decision concerning the admissibility of evidence obtained by police through the violent and invasive abuse of the suspect: "The proceedings by which the conviction was obtained do more than offend some fastidious squeamishness or private sentimentalism about combating crime too energetically. This is conduct that shocks the conscience... They are methods too close to the rack and the screw to permit of constitutional differentiation."[15] Torture is real, in other words, so long as we are possessed of a moral sense that is capable of being offended. I would put the question, therefore, in the following way: does Jewish law permit the use of interrogative procedures that "shock the conscience" as a means of eliciting information that may prevent a planned terrorist attack and thus save innocent life?

I am fortunate not to be the first to consider this issue. This enables me to use as my starting point an article on the subject by Professor Itamar Warhaftig of the Bar Ilan University law faculty. A member of a distinguished Zionist rabbinical family, Professor Warhaftig is a prominent Orthodox scholar who has published widely in the field of *mishpat ivri*, the academic study of Jewish law. His article offers a sustained argument that *halakhah* permits the torture of security detainees suspected of involvement in terrorist activity. We are indebted to Professor Warhaftig for helping us to identify the relevant texts and for suggesting lines of thinking and analysis to help clarify the issues. At the same time, we shall see he takes an approach that liberal Jews – and, I think, not *only* liberal Jews – will find troubling and problematic. I therefore, intend to critique his work, but I hasten to add that I intend no disrespect thereby. As one who has come to this subject much more

recently than many others, including Professor Warhaftig, I recognize
the value of their pioneering work; in that sense, I am a dwarf who stands
on the shoulders of giants. Yet just as the dwarf for precisely that reason
can see a bit farther than the giant is able to,[16] I think that it is
appropriate for those of us who rely upon the work of our predecessors
to openly and honestly state our disagreements with them. This is
especially true for us, liberals whose outlook upon the Jewish legal
heritage is bound to diverge from that of our Orthodox counterparts. At
any rate, such critique and argument is the way in which *halakhah*, like
every other intellectual discipline, grows and develops over time.

   Torture: Warhaftig v. Barak. Professor Warhaftig's article[17] is
itself a critique; his target is a 1999 decision by the Israel Supreme
Court[18] on the application of torture against suspects accused of
involvement in terrorist acts. The Court, sitting as the High Court of
Justice, found that officers of Israel's General Security Service (GSS, or
Shabakh) were not entitled under the law to employ methods of torture
upon prisoners in their custody. The Court's opinion, authored by Chief
Justice Aharon Barak, centers upon the authority of government agents
to conduct "investigations" or "interrogations" (*chakirot*).[19] This
authority is determined by legislation, both that enacted by the Knesset
as well as international treaties and legal compacts to which Israel is a
party. That legislation, which defines the permitted methods of
"investigation," is formulated against the backdrop of a fundamental
clash between two competing values or interests (*arakhim o interesim*):
"on the one hand, the desire to uncover the truth, so as to achieve the
public interest in the detection and prevention of crime; and on the other
hand, the desire to protect the human dignity and liberty of the detainee."
Neither of these values is absolute; a democratic society is committed to
both, even though they conflict with each other. The rules of
interrogation are thus the product of a balance between the two, a
balance founded upon a proper combination of reasonableness, common
sense (*hasekhel hayashar*), and decency. The rules must permit the
security forces to wage an effective struggle against crime and terror. At
the same time, rules that define and limit the scope of interrogation are
essential to a democratic society; a violation of those rules is a violation
not only of the dignity of the detainee but of the image of the society as
a whole.[20] On this basis, the Court concluded that the law which
authorizes GSS agents to conduct "interrogation" does not automatically
permit them to utilize any and all means necessary to obtain the
information they seek. Interrogation must be conducted according to

existing statutory guidelines, which explicitly include the Basic Law on Human Dignity and Freedom.[21] Thus, "interrogation" is restricted to procedures that are "reasonable" and that exclude such "cruel and inhuman" measures as sleep deprivation, shaking the prisoner, forcing him to crouch in the "frog" position, excessively tight handcuffing, and the like. Further, the Court denied to security forces the use of the so-called "necessity defense," the claim that the urgent need to protect the lives of innocent civilians warrants the use of otherwise illegal measures of interrogation. The Court did make a significant concession on this point: the "necessity defense" might succeed as an after-the-fact justification, shielding security agents from criminal liability if they do resort to torture. It cannot, however, serve as an *a priori* authorization for any and all measures of interrogation. "Interrogation," in principle, must be governed by the rules of law that protect the person and the essential humanity of the prisoner. The Court acknowledged that adherence to these rules may at times hinder the police in the performance of their duties; still, it is the "destiny" of a democratic regime to deny itself many of the weapons that its enemies will readily use against it. "A democracy must often fight its battles with one hand tied behind its back." Nonetheless, the recognition of the rule of law and of the liberty of the individual constitute an inherent element of a democracy's very concept of security, "strengthening its spirit... and enabling it to triumph over all its difficulties." And despite its evident sympathy with those who must fight on the front lines against terror, the Court has a duty to perform; "we are judges, and our fellow citizens demand that we function in accordance with the law." That law does not permit torture as a means of forcing prisoners to reveal information, even in the case of the "ticking time-bomb," when the detainee may possess knowledge of an imminent terrorist strike.[22] The Knesset, of course, as the supreme legislative authority, might alter the law. Yet even that alteration must take into account the requirements of the Basic Law that guarantees the human dignity and freedom of the citizens of the State of Israel.

Professor Warhaftig sharply attacks the Court's decision on the grounds of Jewish law: regardless of the correct interpretation of Israeli law,[23] the *halakhah*, he contends, would in principle allow security forces to utilize torture in order to force a suspect to reveal details of a planned terrorist attack.[24] He bases his argument upon the following grounds.[25]

1. Jewish law would define a detainee who is either plotting a

terrorist attack against human targets or possesses information about an impending attack as a *rodef*, a "pursuer" who poses an immediate threat of death to his intended victim. And "when one pursues another with intent to kill, every Jew is obligated to save the victim from the pursuer, even at the cost of the pursuer's life."[26] To this, Warhaftig applies a *kal vachomer* (*a forteriori*) argument: if it is permitted to kill the *rodef* in order to save his victim, then we are certainly authorized to take other measures short of killing, including torture, to achieve that purpose.

2. Warhaftig concedes that the law of *rodef*, strictly speaking, applies only to the situation of the "ticking time bomb," where the danger to life is certain and imminent. It does not apply to a case where it is uncertain that the suspect possesses information that will in fact lead to the prevention of a terrorist attack. We are permitted to kill the *rodef*, in other words, only when we know that this extreme act is the only way to save his intended victim(s). If this is so, then the warrant for torture of one who is *suspected* of being involved in or of having knowledge of a planned terrorist strike, which Warhaftig derives from the *rodef* principle, also falls. Nonetheless, we are still permitted to use torture, because "we are not dealing here with an innocent citizen" but with a silent participant in a planned act of terror, one who if he wished could spare himself the torture simply by revealing the information that in any case he is required to provide under the obligation to save life (*pikuach nefesh*) and to do justice (*dinim*).[27] And, as we shall see, Jewish law permits the coercion of individuals to force them to perform their obligations.

3. These are not normal times. We are at war against enemies who seek our destruction. And during a time of war (*sha'at milchamah*), it is permitted to kill the enemy without concern for such niceties as standard criminal investigative procedure.[28]

4. Jewish tradition commands us to respect the fundamental human dignity (*kevod haberiyot*) of all persons. Yet a terrorist, or for that matter a possible terrorist, possesses no "dignity" that we are charged to recognize. We are forbidden to trample upon the human dignity of the normal criminal suspect, who is under investigation for an act that he has already committed. This

detainee, by contrast, "is being tortured so that he not commit a transgression (*kedei shelo ya'aseh*)." It is entirely up to him to choose to reveal the information, and if he does so, he will not be tortured." He, through his silence, "is the cause of his own loss" (*ihu de'afsid anafsheh*).[29] He has chosen to be tortured, and we are not responsible for that choice.

5. Jewish law permits the *beit din* to coerce individuals under its jurisdiction to fulfill their legal responsibilities. In Rambam's words, the court may "contend with, curse, beat, and pull the hair" of anyone who refuses to hearken to the law's demands. "Likewise, he may bind a person's hands and feet, imprison him, and cast him to the ground." All these acts, of course, must be undertaken for "the sake of Heaven," and the dignity of the detainee must be respected even when harsh measures must be applied against him[30] Still, the language of the *Mishneh Torah* indicates that if torture is the only means by which to induce proper conduct, the judge is empowered to resort to this tool.

6. The Supreme Court's decision underscores the "ideological difference" that distinguishes Torah law from the fundamental assumptions of the Western legal tradition. "In Western culture, there are no sacred values; there is no purpose to life more important than life itself." That is to say, in Western culture there are no objective standards of truth, and in the absence of such standards, the law possesses no criteria by which to establish a preference for any one conception of truth over its rivals. The law therefore shies away from making substantive judgments on questions of value. The ultimate value is individual freedom and tolerance: every person may choose his own path of life, provided that he does not disturb his fellow citizen's right to do the same. These modernistic tendencies have lately been fortified by postmodern thought, which has raised subjectivity "to the highest heights." Concepts such as good and evil have become so thoroughly subjective that today, "in the secular society, it is difficult to speak of any act as 'evil' in an absolute sense." Even if "evil" did have an objective existence, the combined forces of deterministic psychology and Christian dogma (*i.e.*, the doctrine of original sin) absolve the individual of any real responsibility for his sinful actions. The goal of the law is *not* the eradication of evil – such a task lies beyond the conceptual framework of

secular culture – but the purely utilitarian aim to protect society from the acts of antisocial persons. In contrast to all this, the Torah holds each of us responsible for our own actions and charges us as a society "to eradicate the evil from within your midst" (Deuteronomy 13:6 and elsewhere). "The eradication of evil is a religious and not merely social value... In our law, the killing of the *rodef* is not merely excused after the fact; it is an obligation, a divinely-imposed duty." With this in mind, it is absurd to speak of "rights" that protect the sinner against the just punishment that his own actions bring upon him.

Discussion. Professor Warhaftig's essay may or may not reflect a consensus opinion among Orthodox halakhists. It does, however, allow us to see how at least one highly regarded Orthodox academician approaches our subject on the basis of the halakhic tradition. Liberal halakhists are likely to find some serious problems with his position. I list some of them here.

First, as a matter of technical legal analysis, Warhaftig's critique is unfair to the Israel Supreme Court. As a law professor, he should know that the Court's duty is a judicial one: to interpret and apply the existing law, the law as it is rather than the law as the justices or anyone else might wish it to be. Procedures governing interrogations are fixed according to statute,[31] and the Court unanimously[32] found that the legislation makes no allowance for "cruel and inhuman" methods of interrogation. The Knesset, perhaps, should alter the law, but in the absence of any specific legislative act to that effect the justices can hardly be blamed for fulfilling their constitutional responsibility to act *as* justices and not as legislators.

Second, Warhaftig's determination that normal legal protections may be set aside during "time of war" does not distinguish Jewish law from the Western legal tradition. Most modern constitutional regimes make provisions for their governments to assume broad, even draconian enforcement powers during national emergencies;[33] the Torah offers the state no advantages that the secular law does not already guarantee it.[34] That the government of Israel has not decreed such an emergency during the present crisis may or may not constitute a mistake in political judgment. It does not, however, constitute a structural defect in the Israeli legal system or an indictment of modern Western law.

The third problem concerns one of Warhaftig's two major substantive halakhic points: his invocation of the *rodef* principle. At first glance, there is nothing unreasonable about this argument. A person in the process of carrying out a terrorist attack is unquestionably a "pursuer" in the eyes of Jewish law and, to borrow the Court's terminology, of "common sense." Few would object to a security guard's use of deadly force to stop a would-be suicide bomber from boarding a bus or entering a crowded restaurant, and even the "Western legal tradition," Warhaftig's *bête noire*, would not punish the guard for that timely life-saving action. The difficulty arises with the terrorist *suspect*, the one who possesses (or might possess) information about an impending attack to be carried out by others. As has been noted,[35] Warhaftig's classification of the suspect as a *rodef* is an evident *chidush*, a legal innovation. Until now, Jewish law has regarded the "pursuer" as the murderer himself, the one actively on the way to committing the crime. Warhaftig here would seem to expand the concept to include the person who could prevent the murder by revealing information leading to the arrest of the perpetrator but who refuses to do so. The implications of this expansion are far-reaching. Has murder now become a crime of *omission* as well as commission? Shall we follow this logic and define as a *rodef* anyone who refuses to act as a "good Samaritan," that is, one who is capable of fulfilling the *mitzvah* to save life but who chooses not to do so?[36] In response, Warhaftig insists that when the elements of *certainty* and *imminence* are present – that is, when we are certain that the suspect has knowledge of an imminent attack – "he qualifies as a *rodef* even by his failure to act." Yet having made this determination he immediately steps back from it: "At any rate, even if (the suspect) is not a true *rodef* (*rodef mamash*), it is still permissible to coerce him into fulfilling the commandment to save life." Since we are *all* commanded to save life, this formulation effectively removes the suspect from the category of "pursuer" and fixes his legal obligation as that of an ordinary citizen. Is Warhaftig, in spite of everything, uncomfortable in calling this suspect a *rodef*? If so, his discomfort is well-taken; one should be wary of expanding the *rodef* principle beyond its original, tightly circumscribed boundaries. We Jews have but recently discovered to our sorrow that such an expansion can happen all too easily, allowing fanatics to cite the principle as a justification for horrendous and shocking acts.[37] Legal commentators note the same tendency in the contemporary debate – *i.e.*, the debate within legal circles since the terrorist attacks of September 11, 2001 -- over the permissibility of torture by law-enforcement officials. Although governments may assure us that their intention is to use torture only in strictly defined "ticking time bomb" cases, experience teaches that torture is never and cannot be restricted to such scenarios. The conceptual lines are too blurry; the analogies are too inviting; the call of "necessity" guarantees that torture will be applied in cases where other means of preventing an attack are available and even when we are not certain that the suspect possesses relevant information.[38] The *rodef* principle would work in a similar way, serving to justify the use of torture in a variety of cases where "we *think* the suspect possesses critical information, but we aren't sure." The mere *possibility* that the suspect might know something useful would in the eyes of many be a sufficient justification.[39] As one observer puts it:[40]

> Once self-defense is stretched beyond its carefully established, narrowly drawn borders, it becomes a doctrine without bounds. A self-defense argument could be raised to justify torturing a drug dealer who distributed contaminated drugs in order to find out where his drugs are headed. The argument would justify torturing an innocent child in order to compel information from his parent. Torture could be used on someone who likely knows the name or whereabouts of a serial killer. The self-defense rationale, ultimately, would have no limit. In sum, there is a recognizable difference between killing someone engaged in the act of murder, and torturing another person to gain information to prevent a murder.

Warhaftig fails to recognize that difference. Though he concedes that the concept of *rodef* does not truly apply to cases of uncertainty, he has no problem supporting the use of torture in such cases on the grounds that the suspect, even though it is not certain that he has information that can save lives, is a bad person who could easily halt the torture by telling us what we want to know. He is not a *rodef*, in other words, but we will still treat him as one. This circular argument is little more than a sleight-of-hand extension of the *rodef* principle to a situation that, as Warhaftig knows, lies outside its conceptual boundaries. To put it differently, the *rodef* principle is a slippery slope, and Warhaftig has already begun his slide.

The fourth consideration has to do with the other substantive halakhic point in Warhaftig's presentation: his assertion that Jewish law empowers the *beit din*, and by extension the legitimate authorities in a particular society, to employ physical coercion against a recalcitrant individual who refuses to fulfill his responsibilities under the Torah.[41]

The authorities possess this power largely because the individual against whom they exercise it is a bad person who does not "deserve" to be treated with dignity and who could easily escape his suffering by telling us what we wish to know.[42] I want to say something more about this below, but for now I would simply note that the sources Warhaftig cites do not speak of the "terrorist" and do not limit themselves to murderers. Rather, they grant the widest sort of discretion to the court to resort to the physical abuse of *anyone* under its jurisdiction, even the one "who is legally culpable for neither capital nor corporal punishment,"[43] whenever it determines that the public interest demands such action. True, this warrant for government officials to torture (if necessary) a person who refuses to observe the law is not without its limits and controls; the judge may use this power only "for the sake of Heaven" and must at all times respect the basic dignity of the individual whom he is flogging. Yet it is hardly necessary to point out that even the most vicious authoritarian or totalitarian regimes might believe that the torture they inflict upon their opponents is undertaken for good and proper cause, perhaps even for the "sake of Heaven"; moreover, as Warhaftig explicitly declares, the one who refuses to follow the dictates of the Torah possesses no "dignity" that we are required to respect. Here we arrive at yet another slippery slope or, more accurately, at the very end of a precipitous descent: if Warhaftig is correct that governments in fact possess these powers under a Toraitic conception of the maintenance of good social order, then there is no principled way to restrict their application to mass murderers and to those who aid them. Any person caught within the net of the police power, or for that matter anyone who might offend the authorities in some way, would be subject to such treatment, so long as those who inflict it were willing to justify their action on grounds of necessity. This virtually unlimited power of governmental coercion is surely not what we normally have in mind when we speak about the "rule of law."

Finally, Warhaftig underscores the "ideological difference" between traditional Judaism and Western law. This difference, as we shall see, is the pivotal element in Warhaftig's essay, the theoretical basis that upholds the entire structure of his halakhic argument. I want to consider it, in some detail, as an example of what contemporary jurists refer to as the governing "narratives" or "metanarratives" that undergird all legal systems, particular legal institutions, and specific acts of legal interpretation. It is helpful in this regard to compare Warhaftig's approach[44] to that of Chief Justice Barak in the Supreme Court opinion, since Barak, too, encases his ruling within a web of "ideology" – or narrative – that I would contend is essential to his legal purpose.

Let's begin with Barak's opinion. In her study of the Supreme Court's jurisprudence in terrorism cases, Leora Bilsky has noted that the Court "does not limit its decision to legalistic reasoning but also provides a legitimizing narrative for its intervention."[45]

These narratives[46] can be described as 'narratives of contrast,' since the Court compares the terrorist on the one hand and the State of Israel on the other. On the basis of this contrast ('*we* are not like *them*') the Court justifies its refusal to uphold a policy that the security forces deem necessary in the fight against terror.. The limitations [on the use of force - MW] that the Court imposes, in other words, are presented as self-imposed limitations that underline the distinction between a democratic state and its enemies, who do not hesitate to use any means to further their goals.

Bilsky notes that, at the very outset of his opinion, Barak tells a story that establishes a moral contrast between the state of Israel and those who seek its destruction:[47]

> Ever since it was established, the State of Israel has been engaged in an unceasing struggle for its security—indeed, its very existence. Terrorist organizations have set Israel's annihilation as their goal. Terrorist acts and the general disruption of order are their means of choice. In employing such methods, these groups do not distinguish between civilian and military targets. They carry out terrorist attacks in which scores are murdered in public areas—public transportation, city squares and centers, theaters and coffee shops. They do not distinguish between men, women and children. They act out of cruelty and without mercy.
>
> Israel is locked in a life-and-death struggle with enemies who will stop at nothing to bring the state to its knees. Though this grim reality might in the public mind justify an equally brutal response by the security services, the Court urges the Israeli people to rise above their understandable fear and desire for vengeance. Evoking the "destiny" of the democratic state, the opinion reminds its readers that theirs is a society in which the

exercise of official power is limited by the rule of law and a commitment to human rights. We define ourselves as a democracy; as such, we are a society that offers legal protections to the criminal suspect and that looks with suspicion upon every effort by our governmental authorities to exceed the legally-established limits of their power. This means that we are fundamentally different from our enemies. Our deepest ideals and commitments as a society oblige us to deny ourselves a tool of investigation that, however efficient it may be, stands in contradiction to our democratic ethos. This implies that our "no" to state-sponsored torture is not evidence of our weakness in the face of murderous violence but of our dedication to the rule of law. That dedication proves our moral superiority over our foes and will, in the end, guarantee our triumph and survival as a society.

What has Barak accomplished in telling this story? Is this exercise in narrative truly necessary to his judicial role? Some legal scholars, relying upon the traditional distinction between a court's decision strictly construed (the "holding") and everything else that the opinion coveys ("dicta"),[48] would dismiss the narrative sections of the opinion as superfluous to its main business, which is to declare that torture is prohibited under the current statutes governing interrogations. The decision stands by itself and does not need the narrative. The holding, and nothing but the holding, is law properly so called; all the rest is extraneous verbiage. Yet this view betrays a misunderstanding of the way that narrative functions in legal discourse. The stories told by litigants, lawyers, and judges provide explanation and context, purpose and coherence to the legal life and acts of a community. They are not to be considered as frills, as literary embellishments of the true substance of the law, but rather part of and parcel of law itself, the embodiment of the cultural, ideological, and at times theological commitments that make a community's legal thought possible and meaningful. As Robert Cover has memorably put it:[49]

> No set of legal institutions or prescriptions exists apart from the narratives that locate it and give it meaning... In this normative world, law and narrative are inseparably related. Every prescription is insistent in its demand to be located in discourse, to be supplied with history and destiny, beginning and end, explanation and purpose. And every narrative is insistent in its

demand for its prescriptive point, its moral. History and literature cannot escape their location in a normative universe, nor can prescription, even when embodied in a legal text, escape its origin and its end in experience... The narratives that any particular group associates with the law bespeak the range of the group's commitments. Those narratives also provide the resources for justification, condemnation, and argument by actors within the group, who must struggle to live their law.

We should bear in mind, too, that the opinion, the chief literary form of appellate court communication, has always been more than the mere statement of the holding, the legal bottom line. As a genre of judicial writing, the opinion serves as the argumentative exposition in support of the ruling. Its function is an essentially rhetorical one: to explain the decision, to offer reasons for it, to persuade the judge's intended audience to think about this particular question of law in this particular way and to think about themselves as the particular kind of community that the narrative describes or evokes.[50] This task can be performed *only* by means of a consciously employed judicial rhetoric in which the element of narrative figures prominently. At times, the goal of persuasion may be much more difficult to accomplish; in such instances, the narrative elements of this opinion will be expanded and developed accordingly. In the case before us, Barak wishes not only to issue his ruling but to "sell" it to a public that has good reason to question its wisdom. To restrict the investigative methods employed by the security forces might significantly hinder their efforts to foil terrorists. The decision leaves the Court open to the charge that it bears moral responsibility for the lives lost in the next terrorist attack, lives that might have been saved had the police been permitted to "coax" a detainee into revealing what he knew about it in advance of its occurrence. Barak's narrative is a two-fold response to this challenge. First, he openly acknowledges the horrific reality of terrorism, thereby validating the fears and concerns of the Israeli public and cementing a bond of fellow-feeling with his readers ("I am one of you; your experience is mine as well"). Second, he urges them to join him in putting that experience in its proper perspective. Let us not forget, Barak tells them, who we are. *We* are not terrorists. *We* are better than they are. *We* therefore must not sink to their level of violence. In so doing, he gives voice to the higher aspirations of Israel as a democratic society, calling upon his readers to live up to the admittedly exacting standards of justice and political morality that a liberal democratic community proclaims as its ideal. It is only within the context of this narrative, which reminds the Israeli public of the deep commitments that characterize the nature of their polity, that Barak can hope to convince them that they have no choice but to accept the Court's ruling and its potentially grim implications. It cannot be too heavily emphasized, therefore, that the narrative is vital to the success and purpose of the opinion. It may be "dicta," but it is no less *law* for that.

In the same way, Professor Warhaftig's "ideological difference" is a contrast narrative: "we are not like them." In this case, "we"are the Jewish people, at least that segment of the Jewish people that is faithful to its ancient heritage, and "they" are the representatives of the modern Western world, who assume that their culture is moral superiority to one based upon traditional religious values. They have it all wrong; our culture is in fact morally superior to theirs. Theirs is a universe devoid of objective value, in which good and evil have no substantive existence, in which the highest calling is the satisfaction of one's own desires, while we live a life defined by clear standards of right and wrong in which our actions are governed by duty. The centrality of duty in the Jewish conception of morality enables Warhaftig to argue for the acceptability of torture, not only in the case of the "ticking time bomb" but even when the suspect is not truly a *rodef*. This, on its surface, is a difficult point for him to "sell" to his intended audience, among whom are any number of "modern" or "centrist" Orthodox readers who would presumably be disturbed at the specter of police powers normally associated with brutal totalitarian regimes. In order to succeed in his rhetorical purpose, he must galvanize them around the "higher aspirations" of Jewish tradition, especially its primary emphasis upon duty to others over the rights of the individual. We begin our moral thinking from that perspective; the moral life is possible only within a web of values based upon obligation. My overriding duty is to observe God's commandments, among which is the responsibility to save the life of one who is in danger. I have no "right" to refrain from that duty; accordingly, the community is empowered to coerce me by whatever means necessary into performing it. The halakhic permit of physical torture, which on its face would seem to violate the most elemental standards of human dignity, is in fact evidence of the Jewish tradition's moral superiority over Western culture. The point, of course, is that the narrative is absolutely central to Warhaftig's purpose. It is *only* on the basis of this narrative of contrast that he is able to construct a credible halakhic argument for torture. It is *only* when we tell *this* story about

ourselves, our community, and its relation to the world that we are likely
to accept at face value the Maimonidean statement that the government
authorities have the power to "contend with, curse, beat, and pull the
hair" of any person who refuses to fulfill the obligations that the Torah
imposes upon him. For Warhaftig, then, no less than for Barak, the
contrast narrative is no "mere" story, extraneous to his substantive legal
argument. His story *is* law, for in the absence of that story his legal
argument would lose its coherence, its ultimate sense.

        Liberal Halakhah: What Is Our Narrative? In both of these
juristic writings, then, narrative plays a crucial and determining role.
Without Barak's narrative rendition of the "distinction between a
democratic state and its enemies," it would be reasonable for a court to
conclude that the established police power to conduct "investigations"
into criminal conduct would by its nature encompass a wide range of
policies "that the security forces deem necessary in the fight against
terror."[51] In the absence of Warhaftig's narrative, an observant Jew might
well be persuaded that the *halakhah* forbids torture as an offense against
human dignity (*kevod ha'adam* or *kevod haberiyot*). Each author seeks
to demonstrate that "the law" says one thing or another about torture as
a law-enforcement technique, but neither of them could accomplish his
purpose without the narrative structure that he creates in his opinion.
Thus, as we liberal halakhists come to consider our own responses to this
question, we would do well to begin by inquiring into the narratives that
we tell in the determination of our understanding of the *halakhah*. What
sort of story do *we* tell about *our* conception of Jewish law?

        The answer is not a simple one. On the one hand, it seems clear
that we would reject Warhaftig's story out of hand; we liberals, after all,
are proud citizens of the Western civilization that he attacks. Yet,
however, uncomfortable we may be with his assault upon the social and
political values of our culture, we are also Jews and, therefore, heirs to
the same Torah that he reveres. We, too, speak the language of *mitzvah*
and duty when we interpret our religious heritage to ourselves and
others. Though our liberal theological discourse may exalt the doctrines
of individual religious freedom and autonomy, as religious Jews we
believe that good and evil are real categories and that individual
autonomy does not entitle the individual to choose evil. When Warhaftig
declares that in the eyes of Jewish law the suspect has no "right" to
withhold information that would save lives, we agree with him: a person
in this situation bears the moral *duty* to speak up, to perform the *mitzvah*

of *pikuach nefesh*, to refuse to act as an accessory to murder. We, therefore, cannot simply dismiss Warhaftig's narrative as the product of an obscurantist medieval mind. Nor, I think, can we liberals glibly assert that we would never countenance torture in *any* situation, no matter the cost to life and safety. Let us imagine a true "ticking time-bomb" case. The police have taken a suspect into custody. They are reasonably certain that he possesses information that could foil a terrorist strike that is planned for one hour from now. If he reveals those details, hundreds of lives will be saved, but the only way to convince him to talk is through the application of severe physical pressure. Are we absolutely confident that, were our opinion sought, we would not approve (or, at the very least, fail to protest) the use of torture in that situation? Even if we stubbornly insist that *we* would never say yes to torture, even in a "ticking time-bomb" situation, we might, nonetheless, concede that torture is *bound* to happen under extreme circumstances, even in the most liberal and civil-rights oriented societies. If such is the case, then realism might counsel that the issue is not how to do away with torture but how best to control and limit its occurrence. As Alan Dershowitz, who has written extensively on the subject, puts it:[52]

> I am generally against torture as a *normative* matter, and I would like to see its use minimized. I believe that at least moderate forms of non-lethal torture are *in fact* being used by the United States and some of its allies today.[53] I think that if we ever confronted an actual case of imminent mass terrorism that could be prevented by the infliction of torture we would use torture, (even lethal torture), and the public would favor its use. That is my empirical conclusion. It is either true or false, and time will probably tell.

Given that torture, to some extent, is inevitable in the face of the threat that terrorism poses to public safety, Dershowitz calls for the introduction of a "terrorism warrant," a legal device that would regularize the use of such methods of interrogation and subject them to judicial supervision. In the absence of such a warrant, he contends, torture will simply be driven underground, and security forces will resort to it in secret without any possibility of control by the courts.[54] A number of legal scholars have criticized Dershowitz over this position,[55] but others have gone beyond him, defending the torture of terrorism suspects and drafting legal arguments to permit it.[56] If lawyers in a liberal society that is ostensibly committed to the protection of human and civil rights are capable of justifying torture, albeit under carefully delineated circumstances, as a weapon against terror, it is not unthinkable that some liberal rabbis, and certainly liberal rabbis working within the ancient discourse of Jewish law, would reach a similar conclusion.

Still, it is difficult to imagine that we liberal halakhists, with all our devotion to the language of Torah and *mitzvah*, would find in Professor Warhaftig's contrast narrative a convincing portrait of our relationship to Judaism and modernity. Indeed, we would see his story as an exceedingly one-sided view of the liberal political culture of the modern West.[57] It is true that some theorists identify liberalism with *libertarianism*, a rights-based ethic that proclaims the supreme value of the individual's right to choose among competing conceptions of the good. Under that conception, the self is prior to any ends that it might choose, so that the only "sacred" and inviolable good is the freedom of the individual to decide for herself just which of those ends to pursue.[58] This, of course, is how Warhaftig understands the moral thought of Western culture. There is, however, a competing approach: the "communitarian" view, which holds that the individual is always situated within a community, a tradition, or (to use the word that has figured prominently in this essay) a narrative that to a great extent constitutes the self and its identity. Where the libertarian proclaims the supremacy of the "unencumbered self" that stands outside of any particular conception of the good, the communitarian responds that we are never wholly separated from the aims and aspirations that characterize our group attachments. Our ethical thinking always takes place from within a web of common meanings and understandings that characterize particular traditions, serving as the starting points of ethical argument and enabling the members of the community that shares that story to arrive at substantive moral conclusions.[59] We liberal Jews exercise our ethical thinking within the context of just such a tradition. We, no less than our Orthodox brothers and sisters, engage in serious discourse over substantive moral values; our liberal Jewish ethical tradition, consequently, cannot be caricatured as a dogmatic commitment to freedom of choice as the exclusive or the only absolute moral value. To be sure, *our* tradition or narrative entails a deep and abiding commitment to the dignity – the *kavod* – of the individual human person. Yet this signifies our affirmation of human dignity as a necessary condition of the moral life: it is only through the acceptance of the concept of human and civil rights that moral values can be realized. We liberals can certainly agree that unrestricted personal freedom and the ceaseless pursuit of selfish desires are not the goals to which morally sensitive people should aspire. We can and readily do declare that "morality" by any definition demands that the end of justice is the construction of a just *society*, a community founded upon mutual concern rather than upon the radical freedom to pursue one's personal satisfaction. But, we would also say (and we think recent history proves us correct) that a society that fails to safeguard the rights and liberties of the individual is a society that is in deepest sense *unjust*. To put this another way, in *our* world, the social, political, and moral universe that we have inhabited for the past two centuries, regimes that have subsumed the dignity of the individual to some "higher" purpose have tended to be the instigators of the most unspeakable atrocities that humankind has ever witnessed. *Our* narrative must therefore begin with the clear statement of contrast: "*we* are not like *them*."

I do not wish to be misunderstood. I do not consider Professor Warhaftig a friend of totalitarianism; I am certain that he would blanch at the thought. In today's world, however, the power to torture detainees, the remedy that he advocates, would not be administered by rabbinical authorities whom God would safeguard from error.[60] It would lie instead with officials whose authority flows not from divine inspiration but from a constitutional arrangement adopted by the people. In Western societies, that arrangement involves carefully specified limitations upon governmental power, particularly when the application of that power would transgress upon individual rights and human dignity. A warrant for torture, in other words, would exact a painfully high price from a liberal and democratic regime; it would call into question that regime's very legitimacy to govern in the name of its people.

Numerous legal scholars have noted this danger, sounding the warning in words too clear and chilling to be ignored. Particularly instructive are some responses to the report of the "Landau Commission," established in 1987 by the government of Israel to investigate the interrogation methods employed by the GSS. The commission found, among other things, that "the effective interrogation of terrorist suspects is impossible without the use of means of pressure... (which) should principally take the form of non-violent psychological pressure... However, when these do not attain their purpose, the exertion of a moderate measure of physical pressure cannot be avoided."[61] To this, Professor Yitzchak Zamir, a justice of the Israel Supreme Court, remarks:

National security is not an end in itself... If in the cause of the struggle for survival we sacrifice the principles of liberty, justice, and peace on the altar of national security, no victory can be more than delusory. There is a form of survival that is not worth the effort.[62]

Others responded to the Landau Commission report as follows.

[The] license to employ physical pressure in interrogation constitutes a victory for terror, which has succeeded in causing the State to stoop to quasi-terrorist methods. The belief that the ends justifies the means, the willingness to harm fundamental human values in order to attain a goal... are salient characteristics of terrorism... An ever-present danger faced by a state confronted by terrorism is that in the course of combating threats... its character as a law-abiding state will suffer.... When the state itself beats and extorts, it can no longer be said to rest upon foundations of morality and justice, but rather on force. When a state (employs) torture, it reduces the moral distance between a government act and a criminal act...[63]

Since World War II, progress has been made internationally to mark the perpetrators of (torture as) outlaws... Any claim by a state that it is free to inflict pain and suffering upon a person when it finds the circumstances sufficiently exigent threatens to undermine that painfully won and still fragile consensus... Lost would be the opportunity to immediately condemn as outlaw any state engaging in these practices.[64]

We would be curious to see the Israeli legislature – or any legislature of a country laying claim to legitimacy – attempt to draft such a "justification" [*i.e.*, for permitting physical pressure in the interrogation of suspects–MW] in its criminal code, even along the "moderate" lines drawn by the Commission in its Report. We are certain it would not display such arrogance. Such an act would constitute an affront to the fundamental values common to all civilized peoples and which cannot be bent.[65]

My point in bringing these quotations is not to claim that all decent people necessarily share this negative reaction to the Commission's findings. Former Chief Justice Moshe Landau and the

other members of his Commission could hardly be depicted as
"indecent," and their conclusions reflect a serious and thoughtful effort
to draw a balance between the rule of law and the need to protect the
public.[66] My purpose, rather, is to suggest that these sentiments have a
special resonance with us. I suspect that we liberal halakhists tend to
recognize *our* story in the words of these critics of the Landau
Commission report as well as in the words of Chief Justice Barak. In our
narrative, the Torah does not stand in implacable opposition to modern
culture; instead, it incorporates that culture's highest cultural
achievements and moral insights. For this reason, we cannot accept an
interpretation of Torah and *halakhah* that would sanction the imitation
of the methods of the terrorists, that would allow us to act, in the name
of "righteousness," in a manner that is "shocking to the conscience,"
destructive of the rule of law and of the very concept of human rights.
Modernity, to be sure, has seen a great falling away from the path of
religious discipline. Its emphasis upon the centrality of the individual is
in many ways at odds, as Warhaftig notes, with traditional Jewish
teaching. We are not blind to this reality. We frequently take our society
to task for its materialism, for its addiction to a technology that often
strangles human values, and for its numerous other shortcomings. Yet for
all that, we liberals believe in *progress*. Modernity has deepened our
understanding of the content of the halakhic principle *kevod haberiyot*
and of the traditional notion that each one of us is created in the Divine
image. These ideals were defined differently during Biblical, Talmudic,
and Maimonidean times. Jews in those days told different stories about
their world and about their place in it, and that world may not have been
hospitable to the ideals of individual freedom, religious and intellectual
pluralism and tolerance, and limited government. We liberals, however,
cannot conceive of a moral universe that does not involve a commitment
to these ideals. And as liberal *halakhists*, we cannot and do not interpret
Torah and Jewish law in a way that lies separate and apart from them.

When we recognize these facts – that is, when we acknowledge
that we always and inevitably interpret our law from within the structure
of our narratives – we learn how to read those texts which, on their face,
run counter to that structure. And this brings me to Warhaftig's citation
from the *Mishneh Torah*, in which Rambam speaks of the *beit din*'s
power to "contend with, curse, beat, and pull the hair" of a prisoner, not
as a legally-specified punishment for a transgression that he has
committed but as an inducement to him to behave properly. The text
does seem to provide an unambiguous warrant for vigorous government

action (read: torture) in the name of morality. I do not claim that the text and the political value system it expresses are totally foreign to liberals. As I have noted, we are not averse to the notion of "duty" as a primary concept in the discourse of Jewish law. And if we believe in such a thing as "obligation," if we are prepared to define a particular act or course of behavior as a *mitzvah*, then we cannot be wholly unsympathetic to the prospect that officers of the law might exert coercive power to induce an individual to perform that which law or morality requires of him or her. I do claim, though, that our own communal narrative – that is, our understanding of ourselves and of the nature of our political community – requires that we deny such a grant of power to the governments of our time. That narrative requires that we read this text metaphorically and not as a literal expression of our aspirations for the world in which we live. By a metaphorical reading, I mean that we might see in this text an expression of Judaism's uncompromising demand for righteous conduct and its concomitant denial that the individual possesses a "right" to deny God and to choose evil. Such a reading would preserve the power and significance of this text and others like it in the world of Jewish thought; it would not, however, commit us to the literal application of Rambam's ruling as a warrant for torture.

We liberals, moreover, have no monopoly on this sort of metaphorical reading. Our Orthodox co-religionists do it as well. As an example, let us consider a legal issue quite similar to the one we are discussing here. I have in mind the law concerning the recalcitrant husband, the man who refuses to issue a divorce to his wife even when the *halakhah* would require that he do so. Since the law requires that a document of divorce (*get piturin*) must be issued of the husband's free will and consent,[67] he is by that very fact empowered, through his refusal to grant that consent, to render his wife an *agunah*, that is, to deny her the right to remarry. Yet the *halakhah* also provides that on certain grounds a rabbinical court may both require that a husband issue a divorce and coerce him, with whips if need be, to obey its decree.[68] Although this provision seems a logical absurdity – how, after all, can a person be coerced into doing something "of his own free will"?[69] – it is justified by the theory that this coercion is simply a means by which to subdue the husband's evil impulse, which is preventing him from acting upon his natural desire to adhere to the Torah and to the instructions of the Sages.[70] This theory was clearly developed as a positive response to an evident injustice and a clear abuse by a husband of the powers granted to him by the law. If administered energetically, it would likely offer as effective remedy to the plight of many *agunot*. Nonetheless, the Orthodox rabbinical courts today do not utilize physical coercion as a means of inducing a husband to divorce his wife. Even in Israel, where state law empowers the *beit din* to exercise coercive power in such cases, that grant of power extends only to imprisonment of the husband, the revocation of his passport or driver's license and the imposition of other disabilities. The judges are not permitted to beat him, even though the halakhic sources would allow them to do just that.[71] Orthodox scholars tend to explain this stance on the grounds that physical coercion, when used inappropriately, might invalidate the husband's expressed statement of consent.[72] This explanation, however, raises more questions than it answers. What, after all, is the *essential* difference between physical coercion, which is prohibited under contemporary law and rabbinical practice, and non-physical coercion, which the law permits? Both sorts of inducement involve the exertion of unwanted and unpleasant pressure upon the husband as a means of forcing him to do something that in the absence of such measures he would not do. It would seem that a more elemental distinction is at work. Although the rabbinate is not opposed to coercion per se, it is disturbed by the specter of *physical* coercion. To put this in contemporary legal language: in the legal culture of a civilized society, the application of physical force as a means of compelling an individual to do the right thing is an act "that shocks the conscience." The authorities refrain from using it, even though they do allow themselves other forms of coercive pressure, and even though in doing so they deprive themselves of a powerful tool for the attainment of a just result, precisely because "we are better than that." They see themselves as representing a *just* society, and such a society is one that recoils from remedies of this sort. In other words, the law of physical coercion remains on the books, but we no longer act in accordance with its terms. The community's *narrative*, its understanding of the nature of its law and of the purposes it is meant to serve, denies the law its literal application.

All of this suggests that Jews no longer understand their world in accordance with the plain sense of that Maimonidean text; rabbis, including Orthodox rabbis, no longer accept torture as a force for social good, a legitimate instrument of government power. Our ancestors may have lived in a different world, one where the *beit din* wielded (at least in theory) virtually unlimited coercive power over disobedient citizens. For them, it may have been a foregone conclusion that the end, so long as it was required by the Torah, justified the application of violent means in order to secure it. In our day and age, we are loathe to vest this sort of power in the hands of our political leaders. There may have been a time when the employment of a virtually unlimited range of coercive measures served the interests of justice; today, as I have indicated, the phenomenon is tightly associated in our minds with the most degraded and contemptible regimes on earth. None of this necessarily means that Maimonides was "wrong" in his interpretation of the *halakhah* and its Talmudic sources. It does mean, though, that the text, if it is to possess any sort of meaning, must be understood metaphorically, as a symbolic expression of the Torah's absolute demand upon us. But we Jews today do not understand that text, as our ancestors may have done, as a literal warrant for our governments to utilize physical abuse and even torture to compel individuals to toe the moral line. The difference between then and now lies not so much in the words of our halakhic texts but in the narratives with which we convey them, explain them, and provide them with their final justification.

Professor Warhaftig, of course, is entitled to disagree. He may wish to argue for the literal interpretation of Maimonides' ruling in order that it might serve to justify the use of torture against suspected terrorists. At the same time, however, he must concede that the text in its literal sense cannot be restricted to cases of terror and of *pikuach nefesh*. Indeed, Rambam's ruling authorizes the power of judicial coercion over *all* areas of the law and as a means of inducing proper conduct in *any* matter that the governing authorities think important. To apply this text literally, in other words, is to extend its reach to the entire range of human social behavior. Would Professor Warhaftig take the *halakhah* to such a point? Would he, in the name of Jewish law, grant to his government the power to bring coercive physical pressure upon any "wrongdoer" – tax evaders, deadbeat parents, habitual violators of traffic laws, individuals who do not contribute their fare share to *tzedakah* – to toe the moral line as defined by the dominant groups in the society? I do not think that he would want to live in that kind of repressive society. I believe that, were it up to him, he would limit the power of torture to cases where life is truly in danger. Yet the text upon which he relies makes no such limitation. Ultimately, I think that Professor Warhaftig would want us to read Rambam's ruling literally, yes, but only to a certain point. To justify such a novel strategy for interpreting the text, he would have to rely upon some theory of interpretation that is based upon our fundamental values, upon our notion of ourselves as an organized society. That theory would be a narrative, the sort of story that we tell about ourselves that instructs us as to the way we read and understand our law.

Toward a Conclusion. For all these reasons, we who represent the ideal of "liberal" or "progressive" *halakhah* have sufficient cause to reject Professor Warhaftig's interpretation of Jewish law as it relates to torture. To return to the question of balance with which we began, we would say that while our governments must wage a tough and vigorous war against those who use terror to threaten human life and the social order, we cannot follow Warhaftig's claim that the Torah and the Jewish legal tradition authorize the government to use torture as a weapon in this war. The *halakhah*, as we understand it, demands that the government maintain its fidelity to the human dignity and the rule of law even in the midst of this struggle. *Our* narrative, the context from within which we do and must interpret the rules of our law, forbids us from mimicking the methods of those who would destroy us. To do so, even in the name of national security, would be to grant them the very victory that we wish to deny them.

And yet... there can be a difference, a profound one, between what we say in the name of our law and what we actually *do*, the way we conduct ourselves in the crucible of reality. I return to a question I raised above: with all our evident dedication to such liberal and progressive ideals as the inherent dignity of the human person and the rule of law, are we absolutely certain that Professor Warhaftig does not in some way give voice to our own sentiments? Even though we reject his arguments, a disturbing question remains: would we liberals *never* support our government's use of torture, no matter what the circumstances, even in a "ticking time-bomb" case? At the end of the day, after all our protestations that "we are not like *them*," I suspect that many of us, perhaps most of us, would rule for torture in such a situation. Even jurists and moralists who oppose torture on grounds of principle can acknowledge the existence of exceptions to the rule. At the very least, they will concede that government officials might well opt for torture and that they would see their action as justified no matter what the law says. If this is so, if good progressives like us cannot categorically rule out the resort to torture in every possible instance, then we might well ask: what good have we done? What value is there in our careful legal analysis and in our invocation of Jewish values if, when the chips are down, we would look past all of that and (in the words of Justice Barak) plead the defense of necessity?

That is a good question, and like all good questions it resists a facile answer. One line of response is suggested by the American jurist Seth F. Kreimer:[73]

> Faced with a threat of mass devastation that can be avoided only through torture, could an American official believe, as a matter of morality and public policy, that she should choose the path of the torturer as the lesser evil? On this question, I am prepared to concede that there is room for debate, as there is room for debate as to whether under extraordinary circumstances a public official should choose to violate any provision of the Constitution. But on the question of whether scholars or courts should announce before the fact that the Constitution permits torture, the answer seems clearer: ours is not a Constitution that condones such actions.

These words embody one of the core doctrines of the theory known as legal positivism, namely the sharp theoretical distinction between law and morality.[74] These two ways of thought, which deal with the regulation of human conduct, cover much the same ground; nonetheless, they are to be kept hermetically sealed one from the other. Kreimer believes firmly that the U. S. Constitution prohibits torture; nonetheless, he recognizes that a public official would feel enormous pressure, from both external sources as well as her own commitment to the protection of innocent life, to use torture in the situation described. His solution is to allow the official to act on moral grounds, to choose to disobey the law when compliance with the legal standard would lead to a morally indefensible result. That choice, though possibly a moral obligation, remains an *illegal* act; the law (in this case, the Constitution) recognizes no "higher" legal authority than its own rules and procedures.

In Jewish law, by contrast, the distinction between law and morals is not so clear and obvious.[75] To declare that the Torah, as we understand it, forbids torture is to make a statement of moral as well as legal force; by contrast, to say that an action is "moral" even though it violates the Torah creates a difficulty for those of us seeking to work within the parameters of Jewish law, however progressively we interpret it. Yet Professor Kreimer's approach might serve to underline for us the fundamental tension that we can perceive between the demands that Torah places upon us and our capacity to realize them in the harsh reality of life. Our existential dilemma is that we know what we are supposed to do and yet we frequently seem to fall short of that standard. We usually explain this discrepancy on the grounds of human weakness or the evil impulse (*yetzer hara*), and we often console ourselves with the thought that "the Torah was not given to the angels."[76]* In this instance, however, the difficulty arises not from some moral fault or illicit desire but from our desire to "do the right thing": we perceive that in order to save the lives of countless individuals, we shall have to make a choice that conflict with our pronounced moral principles. One way to deal with this conundrum is to pronounce ourselves to be realists or pragmatists: "Such is the world in which we live. We cannot change human nature. Our only choice is to do the best we can in the situation that confronts us." Fine with me. However, we also proclaim ourselves to be *halakhists* and teachers of Judaism, and as such, we should be wary of allowing the "real" to blur our vision of the ideal. Our task is to remember that it is the Torah we are interpreting, and when we speak in the name of Torah, we must keep in mind that we bear the ultimate responsibility for the lessons that we teach in its name. What *we* might do when we confront the terrorists of our time is admittedly an open question. But that reality does not alter the fact that, from our perspective and to borrow Professor Kreimer's language, ours is not a Torah that condones torture. To know this will not necessarily rescue us from all moral difficulties. It does give us, however, a firm basis upon which to stand as we struggle with the moral challenges of our age. And that is no little thing.

Notes

1. *United States Code*, title 22, chapter 38, section 2656f (d).

2. I am not claiming that the concept of "rule of law" *originated* in the modern West. Indeed, the ancient Greeks are aware of "the ideal of the state whose authorities act in accordance with preexisting, known laws not arbitrarily or without regard to those laws," even if they do not enunciate the concept in explicit form. See J. M. Kelly, *A Short History of Western Legal Theory* (Oxford: Oxford University Press, 1992, 24-25. For the history and theoretical underpinnings of the concept see Brian Z. Tamanaha, *On the Rule of Law* (Cambridge: Cambridge University Press, 2004). My point is that in the contemporary context, the "rule of law" is the major distinguishing characteristic between democratic and dictatorial political systems.

3. As one popular formulation would have it, "the government shall be ruled by the law and subject to it"; Joseph Raz, "The Rule of Law and Its Virtues," in R. L. Cunningham, *Liberty and the Rule of Law* (College Station: Texas A&M Press, 1979), 5. Raz does go on to say that the formulation is a tautology; a "government"

that is not subject to its own laws does not act as a government in any meaningful sense of that term. He suggests that the "rule of law" must include the observance of a number of specific principles that guarantee the openness of the law, the independence and supervisory role of the judiciary, and the placing of real limitations upon the police powers of the regime.

4. Ronald Dworkin, *Law's Empire* (Cambridge, MA: Belknap Press, 1986), 93. The late Israeli Supreme Court justice Haim Cohn argued that "the rule of law" rests upon three foundations: the subjugation of the political institutions of the state to the supervision of the law; the independence of the judges who interpret and apply the law; and the great deference paid to the life and the freedom of the individual citizen. See Cohn's *Hamishpat* (Jerusalem: Mosad Bialik, 1991), 143.

5. See Haim Cohn, *Human Rights in Jewish Law* (New York: Ktav, 1984), 17-18, as well as *Hamishpat*, 513. Still, as Cohn notes, the existence of a "right" can be inferred from a corresponding duty: the prohibition of homicide, for example, implies a right to life. See below in the text at notes 8 and 9.

6. See *Tur* and *Shulchan Arukh Choshen Mishpat* 2.

7. This is not to say that one cannot pursue an inquiry into Jewish political theory by means of other genres of thought and expression. Philosophers and social scientists, after all, study the history and development of political ideas from the vantage point of their own disciplines. My claim, rather, is that regardless of the discipline, a Jewish political theory must be derived from source materials that the Jews have historically regarded as authoritative on matters of practice and that these source materials are primarily halakhic ones. See, for example, Menachem Lorberbaum, *Politics and the Limits of Law* (Stanford: Stanford University Press, 2001) and Gerald Blidstein, *Ekronot medini'im bemishnat harambam* (Ramat Gan: Bar Ilan University, 2001).

8. *Yad, De'ot* 7:1-4. Note that "gossip" includes speaking about another person even if one's words happen to be true. *Lying* about another to his detriment is defined as *hotza'at shem ra*. The roots of this particular transgression stretch back to Deuteronomy 22:18-19, which prescribes corporal punishment and a monetary fine for one who files a false claim concerning his wife's lack of virginity upon marriage (*hotzi shem ra*). The Rabbis expanded the scope of this offense to include lying about any other person; see *B. Arakhin* 15a. This usage, it should be noted, is a colloquial one, a synonym for "negative gossip"; it is not strictly speaking a crime or a tort, and it carries no legal penalty. One wonders whether Jewish law, had it adjudicated such matters, would have developed a conception of slander or libel as an actionable offense in the same way that it developed a conception of copyright following the invention of printing. On that subject, see R. Solomon B. Freehof, *Contemporary Reform Responsa* (Cincinnati: Hebrew Union College Press, 1974), no. 55, and CCAR Responsa Committee, no. 5761.1, "Copyright and the Internet" (http://data.ccarnet.org/cgi-bin/respdisp.pl?file=1&year=5761). The point here, at any rate, is that all sorts of gossip, whether the information conveyed is true or false, is prohibited by Jewish law.

9. On this issue, see CCAR Responsa Committee, "Privacy and the Disclosure of Personal Medical Information," no. 5756.2 (http://data.ccarnet.org/cgi-bin/respdisp.pl?file=2&year=5756), section 2.

10. Moshe Zemer, *Evolving Halakhah* (Woodstock, VT: Jewish Lights, 1999), xxii.

11. For an argument in support of the intellectual legitimacy of liberal *halakhah* (*i.e.*, that liberal *halakhah* is no less "halakhic" than its Orthodox counterpart), see my "Against Method," in Walter Jacob, ed., *Beyond the Letter of the Law* (Pittsburgh: Rodef Shalom Press, 2004), 17-77, in particular the final section, entitled "The Practice of Liberal *Halakhah*," at 55*ff*. The article is available as well at http://huc.edu/faculty/faculty/washofsky.shtml .

12. Marcy Strauss, "Torture," *New York Law School Law Review* 48 (2003-2004), 201-274.

13. United Nations Convention Against Torture and other Cruel, Inhuman, or Degrading Treatment or Punishment (1984); check and see Part One, Article One. Office of the High Commissioner for Human Rights (OHCHR), http://193.194.138.190/html/menu3/b/h_cat39.htm .

14. European Convention for the Prevention of Torture and Inhuman or Degrading Treatment or Punishment (1987). For a comprehensive discussion see M. Evans and R. Morgan, *Preventing Torture: A Study of the European Convention for the Prevention of Torture and Inhuman or Degrading Treatment or Punishment* (Oxford: Clarendon Press, 1998), 61-105.

15. *Rochin v. California*, 345 U.S. 165 (1952), at 172. In that case, police and physicians strapped a prisoner to a gurney, shoved a tube down his throat and forced him to vomit up some illegal pills he had swallowed. The pills served as evidence to secure his conviction, which was reversed by the Supreme Court.

16. The "dwarves standing on the shoulders of giants" proverb originates, in all probability, with the 12th-century scholastic philosopher Bernard of Chartres. The earliest use of the proverb by a Jewish writer is apparently found in a responsum by the 13th-century R. Yehoshua di Trani. On this, see Yisrael Ta-Shema, *Halakhah, minhag umetzi'ut be'ashkenaz 1100-1350* (Jerusalem: Magnes), 1996, 70-76. The concept is part of a wider and deeper intellectual debate during the Middle Ages over the proper relationship between the *rishonim* and the *acharonim* – the Jewish version of the conflict between *Antiqui et Moderni*, the philosophical conflict over the authority of the past and the right of contemporary scholars to differ with their illustrious predecessors. For a comprehensive study of the expression of this dispute in Jewish literature, see Avraham Melamed, *Al katfei `anakim* (Ramat Gan: Bar Ilan, 2003).

17. Itamar Warhaftig, "Chakirot hashaba"kh le'or hahalakhah," *Techumin* 20 (2000), 145-150.

18. Public Committee Against Torture in Israel v. The State of Israel and The General Security Service, HCJ 5100/94 (hereafter, *Public Committee*). The English text can be found online at the Supreme Court's search engine, http://elyon1.court.gov.il/eng/verdict/framesetSrch.html. For the Hebrew version, see at http://elyon1.court.gov.il/files/94/000/051/a09/94051000.a09.pdf .

19. See especially *Public Committee* (note 18, above), sections 33-37.

20. *Public Committee* (note 18, above), section 22.

21. *Chok yesod: kevod ha'adam vecheruto*, enacted by the Knesset in 1992 and revised in 1994; the text is available at http://elyon1.court.gov.il/heb/laws/adam.htm On the concept of the "Basic Laws" see David Kretzmer's chapter on constitutional law in A. Shapira, ed., *Introduction to the Law of Israel* (The Hague: Kluwer Law International, 1995), 39*ff*.

22. *Public Committee* (note 18, above), sections 39-40.

23. In particular, Warhaftig dismisses the Court's comments on the "necessity defense" as an affront to common sense: if "necessity" is sufficient to absolve the police of liability resulting from rough treatment of the prisoner during interrogation, why should it not be cited in advance as an *a priori* warrant for such tactics (Warhaftig, 145)? The professor seems to overlook the fact that fine distinctions of this sort are the mainstay of every legal system, including the *halakhah*, which frequently distinguishes between the standards of *lekhatchilah* and *bedi`avad*.

24. The Israeli courts are not bound by "Jewish law" or the *halakhah* but by the legislation and precedents of the Israeli legal system. Nonetheless, *mishpat ivri* scholars like Warhaftig have always been interested in charting the points of connection and contrast between Israeli law and Jewish law. This activity is motivated by a frankly ideological bent: the desire that Jewish law should become the legal foundation of the Jewish state or at least that the law of the state should be informed and guided by traditional Jewish legal principles. For a sympathetic overview of the *mishpat ivri* enterprise, see Menachem Elon, *Jewish Law: History, Sources, Principles* (Philadelphia: Jewish Publication Society, 1994), especially volume four.

25. I number these points here for the sake of convenience; they are not so numbered in Warhaftig's essay.

26. Rambam, *Yad, Rotzeach* 1:6. See *M. Sanhedrin* 8:7 and *B. Sanhedrin* 73a, which learns the principle of *rodef* from Leviticus 19:16 ("do not stand idly by the blood of your fellow," suggesting a positive duty to rescue those in danger) and from Deuteronomy 22:26 (the law of the betrothed maiden "who has no rescuer" – if she *had* a rescuer, he would be permitted to rescue her with any necessary means at his disposal).

27. On *pikuach nefesh*, see the preceding note. "*Dinim,*" the obligation to establish courts of law to administer justice, is one of the seven "Noachide" laws to which all humankind is obliged; *B. Sanhedrin* 56b and *Yad, Melakhim* 9:14.

28. Warhaftig cites *Soferim* 15:7 (ed. Higger; 7:10 in the printed editions), which declares that "you may kill the best of the Gentiles during wartime." The text has clearly been emended according to the comment in *Tosafot Avodah Zarah* 26b, *s.v. velo moridin*, which cites the parallel in *Y. Kidushin* 4:11 (66b), in which the words "during wartime" are missing. That would imply that one is entitled to kill the Gentile at any and all times, presumably because as an idol worshiper he is culpable for death under the Noachide laws. The Babylonian Talmud (*Avodah Zarah* 26a), by contrast, rules that we are not to kill the Gentile, though we are under no obligation to rescue him from mortal danger. Maimonides (*Yad, Avodat Kokhavim* 10:1) applies this rule to a member of one of the "seven nations," the Canaanites who occupied the land that God promised to Israel. This would mean that the law does *not* apply to the Muslims with whom the state of Israel is currently at war. On the other hand, in *Yad, Rotzeach* 4:11, Rambam applies this rule to all "Gentiles" with whom we are at war. Warhaftig, who cites Rambam's two rulings (p. 147, n. 9), does not mention the contradiction between them.

29. Warhaftig acknowledges that this Talmudic principle applies generally to monetary matters (see *B. Ketubot* 2b, 56a, and 89b, among other places). Nonetheless, he asserts, it applies as well to our case.

30. See *Yad, Sanhedrin* 24:8-10. Rambam apparently derives this rule from *B. Sanhedrin* 46a, and see *Tur* and *Shulchan Arukh Choshen Mishpat* 2.

31. See *Public Committee* (note 18, above), section 18, for a listing of the specific legislative provisions.

32. Justice Y. Kedmi filed a concurring opinion. While he asserts that a state has the "natural right" (*zekhut tiv`it*) to protect itself and therefore should find a way to permit coercive interrogation tactics in the admittedly rare instance of the "ticking time bomb," he agrees with Chief Justice Barak and the other seven justices that the existing legislation does not authorize them.

33. "In any civilized society the most important task is achieving a proper balance between freedom and order. In wartime, reason and history both suggest that this balance shifts to some degree in favor of order – in favor of the government's ability to deal with conditions that threaten the national well-being"; William

Rehnquist, *All The Laws But One: Civil Liberties in Wartime* (New York: Vintage Books, 2000), 222.

34. This is not the place (and I am not the person) to conduct a discussion of the laws of war in modern society. I would simply mention, from among all the sources that could be cited, an article by John C. Yoo and James C. Ho, "The Status of Terrorists," *Virginia Journal of International Law* 44 (2003-2004), 207-228. The authors argue that captured Al Qaeda and Taliban fighters do not qualify for the status of prisoners of war under accepted international standards. If this argument is accepted – and the government of the United States has by all accounts accepted it -- it would strip the prisoners of numerous rights and subject them to rough treatment, though not necessarily torture. I present this material, not necessarily because I agree with Yoo and Ho, but in order to demonstrate the extent to which Western law permits a government to undertake extraordinary powers during wartime.

35. R. Yisrael Rosen, in Warhaftig (note 17, above), at 146, n. 3. Warhaftig responds below in that same note. Both Rosen and Warhaftig are editors of *Techumin*.

36. See note 26 and the sources related to Leviticus 19:16, as well as Aaron Kirschenbaum, "The 'Good Samaritan' and Jewish Law," *Diné Israel* 7 (1976), 7-86.

37. See Chaim Povarsky, "The Law of the Pursuer and the Assassination of Prime Minister Rabin," in E. A. Goldman, ed., *Jewish Law Association Studies*, vol. 9 (Atlanta: Scholars Press, 1997), 161-198.

38. For an excellent analysis of the problem see David Luban, "Liberalism, Torture, and the Ticking Bomb," *University of Virginia Law Review* 91 (2005), 1425-1461. From the efforts of the U.S. government to defend its conduct during the current "War on Terror," he concludes that "the liberal ideology of torture, which assumes that torture can be neatly confined to exceptional ticking-bomb cases and surgically severed from cruelty and tyranny, remains a dangerous delusion" (1461).

39. See Strauss (note 12, above), at 262-264: "But torture need not always be effective to be justified... While, undoubtedly, there is ample evidence that torture frequently yields false confessions, this concern is less significant when the purpose of an interrogation is to obtain information and not to secure a conviction... The possibility of even a germ of truth coming from the mouth of an otherwise silent conspirator, conceivably, might be worth the risk... Even if nine times out of ten, a tortured suspect would falsely confess to a crime, or lie to stop being tortured, if the one time truth prevails is the situation where a terrorist has hidden a nuclear bomb in a major city, torture could arguably be seen as effective."

40. Strauss (note 12, above), 260-261.

41. Warhaftig extends this concept of legal responsibility to the non-Jew, who as a "son of Noah" is required to act in accordance with the basic principles of justice (*dinim*); see above at note 27.

42. Warhaftig, at 148: *mi she `over `al hachok...ein lo kavod kelal*, and *"makin oto `ad shetetzei nafsho" (B. Ketubot 86a), shekhen beyado lehafsik et sivlo.*

43. *Yad, Sanhedrin* 24:4.

44. Warhaftig, of course, does not write a formal judicial opinion in *Techumin*, yet his article presents itself as the equivalent of one for all practical purposes: "This is how I would rule on the question at hand from the standpoint of Jewish law."

45. Leora Bilsky, "Suicidal Terror, Radical Evil, and the Distortion of Politics and Law," *Theoretical Inquiries in Law* Tel Aviv University Faculty of Law) 5 (2002), at 153-154. Bilsky is a member of the Tel Aviv University law faculty.

46. In addition to *Public Committee* (note 18, above), Bilsky refers here to *Ajuri v. IDF Commander in Judea and Samaria*, HCJ 7015/02, and *Anonymous Persons v. Minister of Defense*, Cr.A. 7048/97. In all three cases, Chief Justice Barak wrote the Court's opinion.

47. *Public Committee* (note 18, above), sec. 1.

48. See, in general, Mark Washofsky, "Taking Precedent Seriously: On *Halakhah* As A Rhetorical Practice," in Walter Jacob and Moshe Zemer, eds., *Re-examining Progressive Halakhah* (New York: Berghahn Books, 2002), 1-70; available at http://huc.edu/faculty/faculty/washofsky/takingprecedentseriously.pdf .

49. Robert Cover "*Nomos* and Narrative," *Harvard Law Review* 97 (1983), at 4-5 and 46. See also Michael Sandel, *Democracy's Discontent: America in Search of a Public Philosophy* (Cambridge, MA: Harvard University Press, 1996), 350-351: "political community...depends on the narratives by which people make sense of their condition and interpret the common life they share... without narrative there is no continuity between present and past, and therefore no responsibility, and therefore no possibility of acting together to govern ourselves." The subject of narrative jurisprudence is sufficiently complex that I hesitate to offer any discussion here beyond the sketchy indications in the text. For my most sustained effort to date, see Mark Washofsky, "Responsa and Rhetoric: On Law, Literature, and the Rabbinic Decision," *Pursuing the Text: Studies in Honor of Ben Zion Wacholder*, London, Sheffield Press, 1994, at 373-375. The reader might consult the collection edited by Peter Brooks and Paul Gewirtz, *Law's Stories: Narrative and Rhetoric in the Law*. New Haven: Yale University Press, 1996.

50. See, in general, James Boyd White, "What's An Opinion For?" *University of Chicago Law Review* 62 (1995), 1363-1369.

51. See the citation from Bilsky at note 45, above. One obvious way of arriving at this conclusion is the argument, advanced by Justice Kedmi in his concurring opinion (see note 32, above), that a state has a "natural right" to protect itself and its citizens. See as well the Landau Commission Report, cited below at note 61, which argues for the allowance of a moderate level of physical pressure in the interrogation of security detainees.

52. Alan M. Dershowitz, "The Torture Warrant: A Response to Professor Strauss," *New York Law School Law Review* 48 (2003), 275-294. The citation is at 277; the italics are in the original. For a more extended discussion see Alan M. Dershowitz, *Why Terrorism Works: Understanding the Threat, Responding to the Challenge* (New Haven: Yale University Press, 2002), 131-163.

53. Dershowitz goes on to cite numerous examples of the use of torture methods by the United States and its allies against terrorism suspects.

54. "While we abhor the detailed medieval codes and procedures on torture, we ought to recognize that the practice remains. By refusing to discuss torture, we do not make it go away; we drive it underground"; Oren Gross, "Are Torture Warrants Warranted? Pragmatic Absolutism and Official Disobedience," *Minnesota Law Review* 88 (2003-2004), at 1554.

55. See Luban (note 38, above); Strauss (note 12, above); Seth F. Kreimer, "Too Close to the Rack and the Screw: Constitutional Constraints on Torture in the War on Terror," *University of Pennsylvania Journal of Constitutional Law* 6 (2003), 278-325; Jeremy Waldron, "Torture and Positive Law," *Columbia Law Review* 105 (2005), 1681-1750; John Kleinig, "Ticking Bombs and Torture Warrants," *Deakin Law Review* 10 (2005), 614-627. Jeffrey F. Addicott, "Into the Star Chamber: Does the United States Engage in the Use of Torture or Similar Illegal Practices in the War on Terror?" *Kentucky Law Journal* 92 (2003-2004), 849-912, seeks a balanced approach that recognizes the need to infringe on some civil liberties during a time of threat to national security but insists that torture be outlawed.

56. See Memorandum from John C. Yoo, Deputy Assistant Attorney General. U.S. Department of Justice Office of Legal Counsel, to Alberto R. Gonzales, Counsel to the President (August 1, 2002), Karen J. Greenberg and Joshua L. Dratel, eds., *The Torture Papers: The Road to Abu Ghraib* (New York: Cambridge University Press, 2005), 172ff. Yoo is currently a professor at the University of California Law School. The head of the Office of Legal Counsel, who signed the memo, was Jay Bybee, now a judge on the Ninth Circuit U.S. Court of Appeals. See also Mirko Bagaric and Julie Clarke, "Not Enough Official Torture in the World? The Circumstances in Which Torture Is Morally Justifiable," *University of San Francisco Law Review* 39 (2004-2005), 581-616.

57. On the following discussion see Michael Sandel, ed., *Liberalism and Its Critics* (New York: NYU Press, 1984). I employ a somewhat different terminology than does Sandel. He uses the word "liberal" to denote the rights-based theory of ethics, founded upon Immanuel Kant's rejection of utilitarianism. The opposing point of

view, "communitarianism," is *not* "liberal" in Sandel's formulation. I apply the concept "liberal" more broadly to cover both approaches; thus, one might be a "libertarian liberal" or a "communitarian liberal."

58. For a powerful statement of this view see Isaiah Berlin, "Two Concepts of Liberty," in his *Four Essays on Liberty* (Oxford: Oxford University Press, 1969), 118-172.

59. See especially Alisdair MacIntyre, *After Virtue* (Notre Dame: University of Notre Dame Press, 1981), 222: "A living tradition then is an historically extended, socially embodied argument, and an argument precisely in part about the goods which constitute that tradition."

60. For the sake of illustration, see the comment of Nachmanides (Ramban) to Deuteronomy 17:11, "do not deviate from the word that they [*i.e.*, the supreme judicial authorities] tell you, neither to the right nor to the left." A frequent interpretation of the passage suggests that the duty to hearken to the judges' ruling applies "even should they tell you that the right (hand) is the left and the left is the right" (*Sifre Deuteronomy*, ch. 154 and Rashi to Deut. 17:11 – but compare *Y. Horayot* 45d, and see *Torah Temimah* to Deut. 17, n. 62). The penalty for public dissent from the judges' decision is death. Ramban explains the necessity for such a rule of strict obedience: namely, the need for uniformity of interpretation in the law. As for the obvious objection that the judges might be mistaken in their decision and, perhaps, condemn an innocent person to death, Ramban replies that since God's love will never forsake those who serve Him, "they will be preserved from error" (*cf.* Ps. 37:28). Shall we say the same for the appointed judges of our own day, let alone the security officials who would not be required to consult with judges prior to torturing a terrorist suspect?

61. "Commission of Inquiry Into the Methods of Investigation of the General Security Service Regarding Hostile Terrorist Activity," excerpted in *Israel Law Review* 23 (1989), 146-188. The citation is at 184.

62. Yitzchak Zamir, "Human Rights and National Security," *Israel Law Review* 23 (1989), 375-406. The citation is at 379-380.

63. Mordecai Kremnitzer, "The Landau Commission Report: Was the Security Service Subordinated to the Law, of the Law to the Needs of the Security Service?" *Israel Law Review* 23 (1989), 216-279. The passage cited is at 263- 264.

64. Sanford Kadish, "Torture, the State, and the Individual," *Israel Law Review* 23 (1989), 345-356. The citation is at 352.

65. S. Z. Feller, "Not Actual 'Necessity' But Possible 'Justification'," *Israel Law Review* 23 (1989), 201-215. The citation is at 213.

66. Indeed, several of the articles in volume 23 of the *Israel Law Review* devoted to the subject are supportive of the Commission's recommendations.

67. See *B. Gitin* 49b and *Yad, Gerushin* 1:2.

68. See, among other places, *M. Gitin* 9:8 and *B. Gitin* 88b.

69. The classic formulation, *kofin oto ad sheyomar rotzeh ani* ("we coerce him until he says 'I will do it willingly'"), is found in *M. Arakhin* 5:6.

70. *Yad, Gerushin* 2:20, Rambam's elaboration upon the Talmudic formulation "it is a *mitzvah* to heed the words of the Sages" (*B. Bava Batra* 48a and elsewhere). The idea in both texts is that the Jew's *true* desire is to adhere to the *mitzvot*, so that the judicially-imposed coercion simply enables him to overcome his weaknesses and realize that desire.

71. *Law Concerning the Jurisdiction of Rabbinical Courts (Marriage and Divorce)*, 1953, paragraph 6, as amended 2000. See Shelomo Daichovsky, "Akhifat gerushin," *Techumin* 25 (2005), 132-148.

72. The *halakhah* permits coercion of divorce only on certain carefully specified grounds. A divorce coerced for improper reasons is invalid (a *get me`useh*; see *B. Gitin* 88b; *Yad, Gerushin* 2:20; *Shulchan Arukh Even Ha`ezer* 134:7). Thus, the tendency among the *poskim* for centuries has been to avoid exerting physical pressure upon the husband. The classic statement is by Isserles, *Sulchan Arukh Even Ha`ezer* 154:21: "since there is a dispute among the authorities, it is best to rule strictly and not to coerce 'with whips', so that the *get* not be coerced in an invalid manner." He does, however, permit other forms of legal and moral pressure against the recalcitrant husband. One of the best treatments of the subject is Zorach Warhaftig (father of Itamar), "Kefi'at get lehalakhah ulema`aseh," *Shenaton hamishpat ha`ivri* 3-4 (1976-1977), 153-216; see especially at 157-159.

73. Kreimer, note 55, above, at 324-325.

74. The literature on legal positivism is immense. On the particular issue I raise here, see H. L. A. Hart, "Positivism and the Separation of Law and Morals," *Harvard Law Review* 71 (1958), 593-629, reprinted in H. L. A. Hart, *Essays in Jurisprudence and Philosophy* (Oxford: Clarendon Press, 1983), 49-87. For a memorable formulation see Oliver Wendell Holmes, Jr., "The Path of the Law," *Harvard Law Review* 10 (1897), 457-478.

75. This topic is too complex to discuss in any depth here. The complexities *are* discussed in Aharon Lichtenstein, "Does Jewish Tradition Recognize An Ethic Independent of Halakha?" in Marvin Fox, ed., *Modern Jewish Ethics* (Columbus: Ohio State University Press, 1975), 62-88.

76. *B. Berakhot* 25b and *Me`ilah* 14b.

MARTYRDOM: SUICIDE FOR THE SAKE OF HEAVEN

Michael S. Stroh

W e live in a period of time when religious martyrdom has become an important issue, and there is more discussion of martyrdom now than at any time since the Middle Ages. It is obvious why. When people are willing to commit suicide in order to kill others and claim it is an act that God wants, and even commands, we must discuss it. Where does Judaism stand on the question of suicide for the sake of heaven? It is not my intention to present a complete survey of martyrdom in the Jewish tradition or the halakhic parameters of sacrificing one's life for the sanctification of the Name. For example, I will not deal with the martyrs of Masada or the question of whether Samson was a suicide martyr. The common dictionary definition of the word *martyr* is one who chooses to suffer death rather than renounce religious principles. It is not clear with both Masada and Samson that this was the motivation. Martyrdom comes in two forms: involuntary and voluntary. Involuntary martyrdom occurs when the person does not intend to die, but is killed for what the person is, or does, or believes. Voluntary martyrdom occurs when the person seeks death as a positive and praiseworthy act. I will deal only with voluntary martyrdom. In voluntary martyrdom, the martyr chooses death because his/her death is pleasing to God. It is the ultimate sacrifice and expresses the deepest love for the Deity; this expression of loyalty and fealty can be matched by no other. My concern will be a relationship with God in which one believes that God views the suffering of the individual or even the death of the individual as a positive and desirable expression of faithfulness. I will make some general observations, and then move to a consideration of two specific texts, the *Akeidah*, and the death of Rabbi Akivah.

In religious martyrdom the act of self-sacrifice is usually connected to a belief in an after-life which is a reward for the act, although it does not have to be so connected. However, it is clear that in Judaism, Christianity and Islam it is. It may entail a concept of soul and body in which the soul is valued much higher than the body and the body may be regarded as an entrapment or cage for the soul. It may be that the body has no intrinsic value whatever; the body is something to be endured until we can leave it and attain blessed relief. The body, perhaps, created by a malevolent god or demi-urge is the seat of all evil. For example, in Gnosticism, escape from the body, which is the source of evil, corruption and suffering, is a goal of the system.

In the Jewish tradition praise is given to those *she masru et nafsham al kiddush hashem,* those who sacrifice their lives to sanctify God's name.

"Said Rav Papa to Abaye: How is it that for the former generations miracles were performed, and for us miracles are not performed? He replied to him: former generations were willing to sacrifice their lives for the sanctity of (God's) name. We do not sacrifice our lives for the sanctity of (God's) name."[1]

The rabbis of Rav Papa's day were being told that they were unworthy of God performing miracles for them because they did not have the strength to sacrifice their lives for the sake of the Name. This also reflects the point of view that as time passes, spiritual resources decline; that spiritually, the earlier is always better. The authority of the past is that, in truth, their wisdom was higher, closer to the source, than ours. This contrasts with the modern *Weltanschauung* in which the later is always wiser and better. The ancient sages did not believe in spiritual progress.

There is a consideration of when martyrdom is mandated: "By a majority vote, it was resolved...that in every (other) law of the Torah, if one is commanded: 'Transgress and suffer not death,' they may transgress and suffer not death, excepting idolatry, incest, (which includes adultery) and murder." When the act is public "one must incur martyrdom rather than transgress even a minor precept."[2]

The difference between a private and public act is the principle of marit ayin - the way it appears. If someone sees a great sage doing the forbidden, that person may lose faith and be led to sin. A sage, therefore, should choose death rather than violate even a minor mitzvah.

Four hundred boys and girls were kidnapped to be sold into brothels. They reasoned: If we drown in the sea, we shall attain the life of the world to come. All four hundred committed suicide.[3] We see that martyrdom is praiseworthy in this context even though it involves neither incest nor adultery, but will involve sexual immorality. Also, we note the close connection between martyrdom and the life of the next world.

As Rabbi Hanina ben Teradion was being burnt at the stake by the Romans: "The executioner then said to him: "Rabbi, if I raise the flame and take away the tufts of wool from over your heart, will you cause me to enter into the life to come? Yes, he replied. …He thereupon raised the flame and removed the tufts of wool from over his heart, and his soul departed speedily. The executioner then jumped and threw himself into the fire. And a *bat kol* exclaimed: Rabbi Hanina ben Teradion and the executioner have been assigned to the world to come."[4]

This story has some resemblance to Luke 23: 39-43 in which Jesus assures one of the two criminals crucified with him that he would have a place with him in Paradise. Hanina ben Teradion is unwilling to do anything to hasten his death, that would be suicide. Suicide and martyrdom are not the same, even when being burnt at the stake. God would take him, when God determined. The executioner (I assume the executioner was not Jewish), however, can do things to hasten death, a kind of *shabbes goy* in extreme circumstances. While Hanina ben Teradion is an involuntary martyr, the executioner who has acquired the world to come is a voluntary martyr. It is, also, interesting that the text believes that a Talmudic sage can confer the world to come at will.

Let us now proceed to the first of the two texts to be considered the, *akeidah*. There are two traditions, one that Isaac was thirteen at the time of the *Akeidah*, another that he was thirty-seven. If Isaac were thirteen years old when Abraham brings him to his sacrifice, then we would consider him an involuntary martyr. But, if he were thirty-seven years old, and behaved the way he did in many midrashic stories, we would classify him a voluntary martyr. To give just one example from Midrash Rabbah:

"...I am now thirty-seven years old, yet if God desired of me that I be slaughtered, I would not refuse.' Said the Holy Blessed One, 'This is the moment!' Straight away, God did prove Abraham."[5]

The *Akeidah* becomes the model for martyrdom and it is no coincidence that Christianity sees Isaac as an adumbration of Jesus. In the Midrash, Isaac's martyrdom is seen as a voluntary and praiseworthy act in obedience to the will of God. In another midrash:

"...Rabbi Isaac said: When Abraham wished to sacrifice his son Isaac, he said to him: 'Father, I am a young man and am afraid that my body may tremble through fear of the knife and I will grieve you, whereby the slaughter may be rendered unfit and this will not count as a real sacrifice; therefore bind me very firmly...'"[6]

Obedience to the absolute will of God, no matter what is demanded, is the meaning of serving God. It may even contradict human feeling; so Abraham, with tears in his eyes is ready to obey God's will, which is a privilege granted to him.[7] ..."R. Azaria said: It is unnatural. It is unnatural that he should slay his son with his own hand..."[8] In Kierkegaard's *Fear and Trembling*, of course, it is the very unnaturalness of the act that moves Abraham from the ethical to the religious stage of existence and makes Abraham the knight of faith. Kierkegaard raises the question of whether there can be a "teleological suspension of the ethical". Under ordinary conditions, slaughtering your son is murder; this is an ethical universal and applies to all people, in all circumstances, in all places, and all times. Is it possible that God might move Abraham beyond the universal and demand a personal act in which Abraham, as a single one, relates to God as one particular person to the Absolute? This would be incomprehensible since only a universal can be comprehended; a particular can never be comprehended. Abraham can explain this command, therefore, to no one since he cannot bring it under a universal. That is why he cannot tell Sarah what he his doing and lied to his servants when he said that both he and Isaac would return from the mountain. The Torah credits human beings with a natural sense of justice. Thus, when Abraham had the famous dispute with God over the destruction of Sodom and Gomorrah, he challenged God by asking whether the judge of all the earth would act unjustly.[9]

Abraham did not need Divine revelation to ask this question. For God to command a person to violate his God given sense of justice, as in the *Akeidah*, presents us with a theological dilemma, and may bring us back to Kierkegaard. We might doubt, however, that the Torah thinks in these terms, and relates to a concept of ethical universals. The sacrifice of the universal may not be part of the Torah story. The Torah may believe that God *can* command human sacrifice, but chooses not to. In the Midrash, Isaac offers himself for slaughter with zeal because this is the ultimate service of God and the ultimate obedience. What I am most interested in here, is not the justice of Abraham making Isaac into an involuntary martyr through obedience to the will of God, but the midrashic Isaac who is a willing and even zealous voluntary martyr.

The Rabbis do find such voluntary martyrdom positive:
" Rabbi Akiva was being judged before the wicked Tunius Rufus. The time for reciting the *shema* arrived. He began to recite it and smile. He said to him: ' Old man, old man, either you are deaf, or you make light of suffering. He said...' neither am I deaf, nor do I make light of suffering, but all my life I have read the verse: " And you shall love the Lord your God with all your heart, and with all your soul and with all your property." I have loved Him with all my heart and I have loved him with all my property, but until now I was not sure I could love Him with all my soul. But now that the opportunity to love Him with all my soul has come to me, and it is the time of the recital of the *shema,* and I was not deterred from it, therefore, I recite and, therefore, I smile."[10]

Rabbi Akiba is not able to fulfil the mandate in the Torah that " you shall love the Lord your God... with all your soul," until given the opportunity to become a martyr. This is his understanding of the meaning of the verse. Martyrdom, then, is not only positive, it is a mitzvah; and without fulfilling it, a commandment of the Torah is not performed.

It is my contention that voluntary martyrdom is an act of sacred violence that is, in fact, a ritual sacrifice. In *Totem and Taboo* Sigmund Freud understands an act of violence, murder, as the founding act of religion and civilization. This act becomes the basis for sacrifice. For Freud, human existence is a perpetual war of the forces of life and the forces of death. So Freud tells us in *Civilization And Its Discontents:*

> " The existence of this inclination to aggression, which we can detect in ourselves and justly assume to be present in others, is the factor which disturbs our relations with our neighbor and which forces civilization into such a high expenditure (of energy). In consequence of this primary mutual hostility of human beings, civilized society is perpetually threatened with disintegration... Civilization has to use its utmost efforts in order to set limits to man's aggressive instincts and to hold the manifestations of them in check by psychical reaction-formations."[11]

Sacrifice displaces the guilt and aggression onto a victim and it is through the sacrificial mechanism that civilization is held together and is not destroyed by its centrifugal forces. Like the struggle between the *yetzer hara* and the *yetzer tov*, this is not something that human beings will evolve out of. As the Jewish tradition tells us that the Torah was given to us to aid the good drive in its struggle with the evil drive, so Freud suggests that civilization needs a Torah of some kind. Perhaps, in the Days of the Messiah, God will take the *yetzer hara*, out of the world, but in this world the battle is permanent. Since this struggle is a defining characteristic of human existence, we will not be surprised to learn that every human institution, including religion, contains the contest. As a matter of fact, the evil drive can express itself in religious symbols and language. For Freud there is, even, a desire for death, a kind of entropy-wish. As Freud says in *Beyond The Pleasure Principle*:

> " If we are to take it as a truth that knows no exception that everything living dies for *internal* reasons- becomes inorganic once again- then we shall be compelled to say that 'the aim of all life is death.' "[12]

For Richard Rubenstein, the Holocaust was a gigantic act of sacred violence with the Jews as the sacrifice:

> "The Nazi 'final solution' represented one vast explosion of all the repressed forces which in Paganism had been channeled into the controlled and regulated slaughter of one victim at a time."[13]

He prefers Paganism and its controlled, sacred violence to our modern, rational post-Enlightenment civilization. The more rational, the more repressed until the explosion comes. Rubenstein believes that one death is better than six million, so even human sacrifice can be justified.

Mary Douglas sees a pattern in the Torah of warring doublets, in which one is blessed and the other is sent into the wilderness. In Leviticus we have the ritual of the two goats, one is sacrificed (chosen) the other is sent into the wilderness.[14] The same pattern appears with the two birds in the cleansing of the leper.[15] Douglas then sees a repetition of the pattern with Isaac and Ishmael, one chosen, the other sent into the wilderness, and with Jacob and Esau, also one chosen and the other sent into the wilderness. When one thinks about it, it also applies to Cain and Abel, one is chosen and the other wanders. Perhaps, the murder of Abel is a sacrifice. The pattern may, even, underlie the account of Adam and Eve where a state of chosenness in the Garden of Eden is followed by life in the wilderness. With the goats, one is clearly the *scapegoat* and bears away the sins of Israel. But in the other cases, it is not so clear which part of the doublet is the scapegoat and which is not. Being chosen does not necessarily mean the chosen one is not the sacrifice.

The name most associated with the scapegoat and sacred violence, as the foundation of religion is Rene Girard. Girard sees sacrifice and sacred violence as a way that a community heals its disorder:

> " Real or symbolic, sacrifice is primarily a collective action of the entire community, which purifies itself of its own disorder through the unanimous immolation of a victim…"[16]

" By scapegoat effect I mean that strange process through which two or more people are reconciled at the expense of a third party who appears guilty or responsible for whatever ails, disturbs, or frightens the scapegoaters."[17]

For Girard, as for Rubenstein, scapegoating is at the heart of religion, and religion is at the heart of civilization. But as compared to Freud and Rubenstein, he does not believe that scapegoating need be perpetual. James G. Williams says the following about Girard and the Bible:

"... At certain times in human history there have been disclosures that unmask the victimization mechanism that results in sacrifice and scapegoating. Such disclosures are focused and sustained in the Jewish and Christian Scriptures...Girard finds in the Bible the revelation or disclosure of a God who does not want victims, a God who is disclosed in the actions of those who take the side of victims."[18]

In the Bible, evil is performed when we transform that which has been given us for life into death, as when a kid is boiled in its mother's milk. Goodness is enacted when we transform that which means death into life, as is the transformation of a war bow (*keshet*) into a rainbow in the story of Noah, or we beat our "swords into plowshares and our spears into pruning hooks". The struggle of life against death is part of the depth meaning of Judaism. Although in our experience, death always wins, since every living creature dies, in Jewish faith, ultimately, in a way, perhaps, we cannot comprehend, life wins.

For Richard Rubenstein, a scapegoat is necessary to maintain the equilibrium of society. It could be a human victim, and human sacrifice has played this role in history. But an animal victim works and is, therefore, preferred to the sacrifice of a human being. Neither is terrible. What is terrible is the bursting out of the feelings kept down in the pressure cooker, the return of the repressed, which resulted in the ritual sacrifice of 6,000,000 Jews. For Girard, we can escape from the scape-goating mechanism; it is not inevitable. The Bible starts the process by identifying with victims. Rubenstein does not believe this can happen, which, perhaps, is why he calls himself a pagan.

In our day, Martyrdom has become the ideal of extremist Islamism. The victims are the scapegoats in a religious ritual. Its cause is not poverty or nationalism or politics. Its cause is religious and goes back "to things hidden since the foundation of the world," to quote Girard. Martyrdom, as a positive religious act, which is desired by God for its own sake, is a sacrifice in which the perpetrator is also the victim, making himself/herself into a scapegoat. All religions have a dark side because of the *yetzer hara* and it is the obligation of religious people to struggle against the dark side of their own religion. Judaism is not immune to this, as the violence of Baruch Goldstein has shown. We can find the belief in Judaism that voluntary martyrdom is the highest form of service and that without it the mitzvot cannot be fulfilled and we have not succeeded in loving God. The Torah does not have a uniform message and interpretation establishes which message is preferred. This, certainly, was done by the Rabbis. It is our obligation to bring the scapegoat mechanism to an end in religious affirmation. It is time for us to declare that God does not want victims and does not desire the suffering and death of God's creatures as a demonstration of loyalty. There are times when a person who does not want to die must sacrifice a life in order not to violate moral principle, and this is noble. It is the evil of the world that might require such an act. But voluntary suicide as an act well pleasing to God, intrinsically, is not noble. The time has come for us to say that voluntary violence as a religious act, whether perpetrated against others or against ourselves, is not desired by God.

Notes

1. b Berakhot. 20a.

2. b. Sanhhedrin 74a-75a.

3. b. Gittin 57b.

4. b. Avodah Zarah 18ab.

5. H. Freedman and Maurice Simon (ed.) *Midrash Rabbah*, London, 1961, Genesis (*vayera*), p. 485.

6. Ibid., Genesis (*vayera*), p. 497.

7. Ibid., Genesis (*vayera*), p. 498.

8.   Ibid., Genesis (*vayera*), p. 495.

9. Gen.., 18:23-32.

10. P. Talmud Berakhot, 9:5.

11. Sigmund Freud, *Civilization, And Its Discontents*, London, 1963, p. 49.

12. Sigmund Freud, *Beyond The Pleasure*, 1963, p. 70.

13. Richard L. Rubenstein, *After Auschwitz*, Indianapolis, New York and Kansas City, 1966, p. 18.

14.   Leviticus 16:8–10.

15.   Leviticus 14:5–7.

16.   Rene Girard, *The Girard Reader*, New York, 2000, p.11.

17.   Ibid., p. 12.

18.   James G. Williams, *The Bible, Violence & The Sacred*, San Francisco, 1991, p. 12.

All Talmud translations are from *The Talmud*, The Soncino Press, I. Epstein, editor, London, 1948. Midrash translations are from *Midrash Rabbah*, The Soncino Press, H. Freedman and Maurice Simon, editors, London and New York, 1983. Some adjustments have been made in the translations to suit modern style.

REDEEMING CAPTIVES
Some Thoughts on the Halakhah

Moshe Zemer

Corporal Gilad Shalit was captured by Hamas on the border of the Gaza strip on June 25, 2006, 979 days ago. His father, Noam Shalit has met on behalf of his son with heads of State who have visited in Israel and abroad. Gilad has been kept in isolation and allowed to received only one of many letters sent to him, through the intervention of French President Nicholai Sarkozi. Shalit has not been allowed visits by the International Red Cross as required by the Geneva Convention on prisoners of war. In the meanwhile his 23rd and 24th birthdays have passed while incarcerated.

There are contrasting views as to the extent that we must go to ransom prisoners. According to Maimonides, there are many *mitzvot* that we must fulfill in our relationship with our fellows: we must feed the hungry and thirsty, clothe the naked, the save those who are in danger of death. The Rambam states: "There is no precept greater than the redemption of captives, since a captive falls into all these categories of hungry and thirsty and naked and danger of death. Those who close their eyes to redeeming him transgress the command......'do not stand idly beside the blood of your fellow' and nullify the precept 'love your fellow as yourself'" (Lev. 19:18). Yosef Caro emphasized the urgency of release. "Every moment one puts off redeeming captives, where it is possible to do so sooner, is like shedding blood." (*Shulhan Arukh Y.D.* 2) If redeeming captives is so vital a precept, it would seem to be our duty to do so at any cost. Yet, the Mishnah holds that "captives should not be ransomed for more than their value, as a precaution for the general good." (Gittin 4:6)

How do we determine the value of a human being? It may be suggested that one check the price at a slave market. This would appear doubtful in the Jewish tradition. More likely our sages would rely on the passage from the Book of Psalms (Ps. 8:8) "What is man that you are mindful of him and the son of man that you care for him."

Meir of Rothenberg, who was seventy-one years old, refused to allow the transaction for himself, proclaiming that the principal: "Not to redeem captives for more than their value" applied to himself. As a result, he languished in prison for the last seven years of his life. The sixteenth century Polish Rabbi Solomon Luria, confirms the details of this case as follows: "I have heard that the Maharam of Rothenburg, *zichrono l''vracha,* was held in the fortress of Ensisheim in the Upper Alsace for a number of years. The prince demanded a large sum from the communities who were willing to ransom him. But he would not let them do so, for he said: 'One does not ransom captives for more than their value.'"

The ransom which the Palestinians have demanded is the release of hundreds of their prisoners whom the Israel Defense Force has captured. The Israel cabinet has decided not to release those Palestinian prisoners with 'blood on their hands,' who have killed innocent civilians by blowing up busses or other acts of terror. Those who have murdered will very likely murder again if released. Eminent authorities are divided on this issue of the amount of ransom that may be paid. Jewish captive faces imminent death. Nahmanides rejected the opinion that when the Jewish captive faces imminent death "one redeems them for whatever sum can redeem them." Meir ben Gedaliah (1558 – 1616) of Lublin agreed with this position (*Responsa* Maharam *Lublin,* Responsa # 15). In the halakhic debate as to the reasonable price to be paid for the redemption of a captive, in the 16th century David ben Zimra wrote that the criterion should be the actual situation in the world. He ruled that it was not proper to redeem Jewish captives "for more than captives of other nations."

According to the halakhah, we must do our utmost to fulfill the meritorious commandment of ransoming Jewish captives. Nevertheless, there is a limit. We must not endanger others by releasing these terrorists. We must attempt to determine whether submitting to extortion will encourage the terrorists to continue and capture other victims. The cruel choice between the two approaches - ransoming captives at any price or protecting the community has led to a third alternative. Specially trained armed forces made attempts to free hostages. In 1994 a young soldier, Nachshon Wachsman, was held prisoner. The attempt of the special unit to free him failed. His captors shot him. His mother stated that she would wish that her son's murderers go free in order to save Gilad Shalit. We all remember the tragic event of the Olympic Games in Munich. The attempt to save the Israeli sportsmen ended in their death. Supreme Court Justice Emeritus, Mishal Heshin, wrote that our unwritten code of military ethics, makes it imperative not to leave a wounded soldier in the field. This is almost universally accepted, even though it may result in the death of the medic who is treating him. In the situation of the captive, when all of the alternatives are dangerous and unacceptable, what can we do? How do we find the inner strength to continue the struggle?

When all else seems to fail, let us turn in prayer to God, our *Shutaf* in the work of creation and pray to God that we may indeed succeed and praise the Divine One, who strengthens us in this joint endeavor. Blessed Are You, *Adonai*, redeemer of captives.

IS A JEWISH PACIFISM LEGITIMATE ?

Arnold Jacob Wolf

How could there be a legitimate Jewish pacifism if the Bible, and later Jewish literature, are full of what seem to be holy wars? But how can there not be when such leaders as Jeremiah, Yohanan ben Zakkai and Rav Aaron Tamaret (rediscovered by Everett Gendler)and such twentieth century members of the Jewish Peace Fellowship as Abraham Joshua Heschel, Albert Einstein and Leo Baeck proclaimed peace as both the goal and the way? The question seems to be both open and complicated. We begin with the famous passage from the Sifre (42:2 in J. Neusner's translation) which exalts the value of peace:

1. A. "…and give you peace:"
   B. When you come in, peace, and when you go out, peace, peace with every person.
   C. R. Hananiah, prefect of the priests, says, "'…and give you peace:' in your house."
   D. R. Nathan says, '…and give you peace:' this refers to the peace of the house of David, as it is said, 'Of the increase of his government and of peace there will be no end' (Is. 9:6)."

2. A. "…and give you peace:" this refers to the peace of the Torah.
   B. For it is said, "The Lord give strength to his people, the Lord bless his people with peace" (Ps. 29:11).

3. A. Great is peace, for on that account the tale involving Sarah was revised.
   B. For it is said, "And I have grown old" (Gen. 18:13).
   C. Great is peace, for the Holy One changed the tale on account of keeping the peace.
   D. Great is peace, for the angel changed the story on account of keeping the peace.
   E. Great is peace, for a name of God that is written in a state of consecration is blotted out by the water so as to bring peace between a man and his wife.

F. R. Eleazar says, "Great is peace, for the prophets planted in peoples' mouths only the word peace."

G. R. Simeon b. Halapta says, "Great is peace, for the only utensil that holds a blessing is peace, as it is said, 'The Lord give strength to his people, the Lord bless his people with peace'" (Ps. 29:11).

H. R. Eleazar Haqqappar says "Great is peace, for the seal of all blessings is only peace, as it is said, 'The Lord bless you and keep you, the Lord make his face to shine upon you and be gracious to you, [the Lord lift up his countenance upon you] and give you peace.'"

I. R. Eleazar, son of R. Eleazar Haqqappar, says, "Great is peace, for even if the Israelites worship idols but keep the peace among them, it is as if the Omnipresent says, 'Satan shall never touch them,' as it is said, 'Ephraim is joined to idols, let him alone'"(Hos. 4:17).

J. "But when they are divided by dissension: 'They love shame more than their glory'(Hos. 4:18 [RSV])."

K. "Lo, great is peace and despised is dissension."

L. Great is peace, for even in a time of war people need peace, as it is said, "When you draw near a city to do battle against it, you will offer peace terms to it." (Deut. 20:10).

M. "So I sent messengers from the wilderness of Kedemoth to Sihon the king of Heshbon with words of peace" (Deut. 2:26).

N. "Then Jephthah sent messengers to the King of the Ammonites and said, 'What have you against me that you have come to me to fight against my land?' And the king of the Ammonites answered the messengers of Jephthah, 'Because Israel on coming from Egypt took away my land from the Arnon to the Jabbok and to the Jordan; now therefore restore it peaceably'" (Judges 11:12-13).

O. Great is peace, for even the dead need it, as it is said, "And you shall go to your fathers in peace" (Gen. 15;15).

P. And it says, "You will die in peace and with the burnings of your fathers" (Jer. 34:5).

Q. Great is peace, for it is given to those who repent, as it is said, "He who creates the expression of the lips: 'Peace, peace to the one who is far and the one who is near'" (Is. 57:19).

R. Great is peace, for it is given as the portion of the righteous, as it is said, "May he come in peace, resting on their resting place" (Is. 57:2).

S. Great is peace, for it is not given as the portion of the wicked, as it is said, "There is no peace, says the Lord, to the wicked" (Is. 57:21).

T. Great is peace, for it is given to those who love the Torah, as it is said, "Great peace goes to those who love your Torah" (Ps. 119:165).

U. Great is peace, for it is given to those who study the Torah, as it is said, "And all your children will be learned of the Lord, and great will be the peace of your children" (Is. 54:13).

V. Great is peace, for it is given to the humble, as it is said, "The humble will inherit the earth and derive pleasure from the abundance of peace" (Ps. 37:11).

W. Great is peace, for it is given to those who carry out deeds of righteousness, as it is said, "And the work of righteousness will be peace" (Is. 32:17).

X. Great is peace, for it is the name of the Holy One, blessed be he, as it is said, "And he called the Lord, 'peace'" (Judges 6:24).

Y. R. Hananiah, prefect of the priests, says "Great is peace, for it outweighs all the works of creation, as it is said, 'Who creates light and forms darkness and makes peace'" (Is. 45:7).

Z. Great is peace, for those who dwell in the high places need peace, as it is said, "Dominion and fear are with God, he makes peace in his high heaven" (Job 25:2).

AA. Now it is a matter of an argument *a fortiori:* If in a place where there are no envy, competition, and hatred and conflict, the creatures of the upper world need peace, in a place in which all of these qualities are found, all the more so [do people need peace].

But what about biblical law which demands the genocide of all indigenous peoples of Canaan? What about Yahweh's many small and large biblical wars? It is clear from the book of Judges that the land of Israel was *not* cleared of its original population by war or by other means; still violence was authorized against the Canaanites throughout the books of Joshua and Judges and against the Philistines later on. The principal Theological Dictionary of the Old Testament clearly indicates nonetheless that peace is a primary goal of biblical religion.

Overcoming War; War and Peace. It was certainly not a matter of indifference to the ancient Israelites whether there was war or peace. The OT says nothing about war as a locus for the development of manly virtues. War is also full of violence (cf. merely Dt. 20), violence which P was not the first to view negatively (Gen. 6:12f.). Thus the best antithesis to war is peace, and *shalom* accordingly constitutes the fullest semantic opposite of *milhama* (1 K. 20:18; Ps. 120:7; Eccl. 3:8; Mic. 3:5; Zec. 9:10; cf. also Dt. 20:12; Josh. 11:19; 2 S. 8:10; 11:7; 1 K. 2:5; 1 Ch. 18:10; Isa. 27:4f.). 2 S. 11:7 and also Jgs. 8:9; 1 K. 2:5, however, show that – *shalom* does not always mean simply the "absence of war."

It is then especially post-exilic texts (or additions from this period) that speak of peace and hope (often as eschatological promises) that Yahweh will destroy all weapons (Jer. 49:35; Hos. 1:5; 2:20[18]; Mic. 5:9f.[10f]; Zec. 9:10). Originally, this probably meant (only) that he would do this because of and through his intervention in war on Israel's behalf. However, such statements concerning the war of Yahweh (!) were modified and expanded into positive, general anticipation, developing probably from the basis of Ps. 46:10(9) (cf. 76:4[3]). Isa. 41:12 foretells an end to the (Babylonian) men of war, and the promise in 28:5f. (secondary) probably also referred initially only to one quite specific enemy before receiving a more expanded interpretation. According to Hos. 1:7 (addition), Yahweh will no longer deliver through war; yet next to Zec. 4:6 we later have the evidence of 10:3-5 or ch. 14; and even the beautiful testimony of hope in Isa. 2:4 (Micah 4:3) finds not only its antithesis in Ps. 18:35, 40 (34, 39), but also its negative counterpart in Joel 4:10 (3:10), even if according to the context there are those who so speak will come to ruin. The notion of peace among nations was not primarily, and certainly not exclusively, Israelite, nor was such hope able to establish itself as the predominant one within the OT, as shown by the book of Daniel and other texts of early Jewish apocalypticism. At this point one should not be too quick to harmonize, nor to read the OT too one-sidedly in its testimony concerning war and peace. Although as a statement of trust Job 5:20 does indeed occupy a weighty position within its own context, it also finds its direct corrective and counter argument in Ec. 8:8. [Botterweek *et al.* VIII, 342f.]

In contradistinction to the gods of other ancient civilizations, the Hebrew deity is *not* a god of war. Martin Buber, in what is perhaps his greatest book, explicates the distinction:

> JHWH is not, as is frequently understood, a war-god; nor a covenant-god developed into a war-god. War-gods help their fighting peoples. They do not, with human and super-human armies, wage their own wars. The mighty-weaponed Ashur helps Sennacherib against Phoenicians, Philistines and Hezekiah of Judah, but he does not command a war with Judah as JHWH with Amalek "from generation to generation" (Exodus 17:16). The "*baal* of heaven" grants to King Zakir of Hamath power to stand firm against the league of the seven kings under Ben-Hadad of Aram known from the Elisha legend, but certainly Zakir did not feel as one who wages the wars of *baal* (cf. I Samuel 17:47; 18:17; 25:28; 30:26), and the songs which celebrated his victories are certainly not gathered together in a book of the wars of *baal* (cf. Numbers 21:14). The protector-god wages the war of his protégés; the *melekh* JHWH wages His own war. When Deborah says to Barak (Judges 4:14): "Does not JHWH go before you?" she speaks not to the devotee of a cult-numen, but to a follower of a divine duke...

> But the point in time, beyond which, while there are war-oracles and, of course, ritual remains, there is nevertheless no JHWH-war to be found any more in the texts, still has a special significance. It is the moment before those campaigns of David which, by means of the final conflicts of liberation and the subjugation of the last Canaanite enclaves,

complete the work of the occupation (II Samuel 5), and to which in characteristic fashion the beserker-exploits of chapters 21 and 23 also, for the most part, belong, campaigns which are distinguished by expansive undertakings which are narrated by the historiographer either quite cursorily (chapter 8) or in such a way that one perceives clearly the altered character of the leadership (10:12). This moment is characterized in the "Deuteronomistic," but for the direct apprehension of the historical perspective which the one responsible for the narrative context intends, indispensable (anticipating, after all, only verse 11) parenthesis 7:1b as the one in which JHWH "had afforded" to David "rest from all his enemies round about." That is set forth in the following speech of God—which is mostly understood as referring to the future and thereby in its fundamental meaning misunderstood: "I have appointed a place for My people, Israel / I have planted it, / that it may dwell in its own place." One cannot say more clearly that here an era comes to an end, the era of that historical action which we call the wandering and settlement of Israel – and therewith also the era of the JHWH-war. (Buber, *Kingship of God*, pp. 142ff.)

Biblical scholar Susan Niditch describes the paradox of war and peace in these words:

In fact, the history of attitudes to war in ancient Israel is a complex one involving multiplicity, overlap, and self-contradiction. There is more than one variety of ban ideology, and various war ideologies coexist during any one period in the history of Israel. The priestly ideology of war has much in common with the ideology of the ban as God's justice while the violent pragmatism of the ideology of expediency is reflected also in the ideology of tricksterism. Those whose courts produced the ennobling bardic tradition may well have practiced the brutal ideology of expediency. Those who imagine God fighting and not humans thereby planting seeds for pacifists later in the western tradition nevertheless express desires to utterly destroy certain of their own kinsmen. (Niditch: pp. 154f.)

In sum, while there is surely some authorized violence in the Hebrew Bible, much of it, if not most of it, theoretical, it is still true that non-violence, at least by human agency, is most effective. Thus, the end of Egyptian slavery is accompanied by no battles except striking miraculous victories that God wins. Jericho falls without a battle. Senaccherib's invading force is driven back by divine not by human intervention. And great prophets urge non-violence or even absolute non-resistance to foreign incursion. Clearly, the Hebrew Bible is, in principle, at least in favor of peaceful solutions to danger or to threat of danger.

Rabbinic views are, if anything, even more complicated. Some wars, against the Canaanite nations and Amalek, are required wars (*milhamot mitzvah* or *hovah*), that is, religious duties. Some are *milhamot r'shut*, optional, that is to say permitted but not required. What is most crucial, however, is that the Canaanites and Amalekites have either disappeared or are now impossible to identify, rendering obligatory wars moot. Maimonides begins the famous fifth chapter of the section "Kings and War" in his code, *Mishneh Torah*, with the following words:

> 1. The primary war which the king wages is a war for a religious cause. Which may be denominated a war for a religious cause? It includes the war against the seven nations, that against Amalek, and a war to deliver Israel from the enemy attacking him. Thereafter he may engage in an optional war, that is, a war against neighboring nations to extend the borders of Israel and to enhance his greatness and prestige.

> 2. For a war waged for a religious cause, the king need not obtain the sanction of the court. He may at any time go forth of his own accord and compel the people to go with him. But in case of an optional war, he may not lead forth the people save by a decision of the court of seventy-one.

> 3. He may break through (private property) to make a road for himself, and none may protest against it.

No limit can be prescribed for the king's road; he expropriates as much as is needed. He does not have to make detours because someone's vineyard or field (is in his way). He takes the straight route and attacks the enemy.

4.   It is a positive command to destroy the seven nations, as it is said: *But thou shalt utterly destroy them* (Deut. 20:17). If one does not put to death any of them that falls into one's power, one transgresses a negative command, as it is said: *Thou shalt save alive nothing that breatheth* (Deut. 20:16). But their memory has long perished.

5.   So too, it is a positive command to destroy the memory of Amalek, as it is said: *Thou shalt blot out the remembrance of Amalek* (Deut. 25:19). It is a positive command always to bear in mind his evil deeds, the waylaying (he resorted to), so that we keep fresh the memory of the hatred manifested by him, as it is said: *Remember what Amalek did unto thee* (Deut. 25:17). The traditional interpretation of this injunction is: *Remember,* by word of mouth; *do not forget,* out of mind.

6.   All provinces conquered by the king at the decision of the court are deemed a national conquest and become in all respects an integral part of the Land of Israel conquered by Joshua, provided that they are annexed after the whole of Palestine, the boundaries of which are specified in the Bible, has been reconquered.
(Maimonides: "Judges; Kings and [Their] Wars," V:1-6)

Further, Maimonides insists that no war may be declared until and unless peace offers are made to an enemy, which amount to opportunity to surrender. The defeated nations must accept the seven laws of the Noahides, perhaps even their divine source in Hebrew scripture. Nations attacked by Israel must be given sufficient opportunity to flee. No fruit trees may be chopped down during hostilities.

Most important are biblically authorized exemptions from war duty. Men with a new house, a new bride or a new vineyard should return from war. Deuteronomy, chapter 20, also directs that "the fearful and faint-hearted" are deferred, meaning cowards or, perhaps, conscientious objectors. In any case, exemptions in Maimonides are very broad. A "house" includes a stable or a hut. A "tree" includes an inheritance, gift or vineyard. A "wife" may be a virgin, a widow or a divorcee, even a Levirate bride. Alternate service may be required, such as repairing roads or bringing soldiers water and food. Fighters are permitted to eat forbidden foods including pork and to drink forbidden wine.

Maimonides is not a pacifist. Nonetheless, even he must point out how Jewish law releases many men from war and how sharply limited are the wars that are required or even permissible. Peace may be the highest value in Judaism, but it remains fluid and elusive. We do not have a rigorous analysis of the doctrine even in such classic works as George Foot Moore's *Judaism*. But peace is an infinite value; it is proleptically messianic—to its enemies a premature messianism. Peace, especially perhaps in a nuclear age, must be relentlessly and categorically pursued. (Landes, *passim*)

The *Tanhuma* astutely remarks that "the whole Torah is peace, even its wars." As to the "required wars," Maimonides asserts "their very memories have perished." And for optional wars, consent of the great Sanhedrin is required, an institution that no longer exists. Defensive wars may still be optional, but, as recent history proves, a definition of "defensive" is murky and untrustworthy. Defensive war has no biblical warrant, in any case. Ultra-orthodoxy is pacifist because it conceives of Jewish history as in God's hands and "climbing the walls" of self-protection is an act of disbelief. (Schwarzschild, *Shalom, passim*) Like the death penalty, it is fair to say, war may be permissible in principle and yet forbidden in any possible individual case. The important Jewish pacifist Steven Schwarzschild (1924–1989) claimed global significance inherent in the Talmudic doctrine of *mipnei darkhe shalom*, that is, the abrogation of halakhic responsibility for reasons of peacemaking. He held that the structure of peacemaking was binding even when and if it violated normal legal strictures. For the sake of peace we are commanded (not merely permitted) to violate the Torah. It is, thus, in his view, parallel to the principle of saving a life even at the cost of violating important Sabbath *mitzvot*. Peace is preeminent and, for its sake, all else is subordinate.

Eugene Borowitz does not agree. He translates *mipnei darkhe shalom* as not much more than "to get along you must go along," that is, we cut some corners when we must, just to keep the peace. The concept must not, in his view, be understood as a principle of Jewish law but, like several others, a mere modification, when necessary, of customary Jewish practice.

This debate cuts deep, I believe. Do the rabbis simply understand that in the real world some minor changes are inevitable, or are they claiming for peacemaking a superordinate role? Is peace a true first principle or a mere strategic retreat point? A Jewish pacifist may legitimately claim it is more than a detail of legislation but, rather, a crucial and indispensable moral demand. God's name, after all, is peace.

Jewish pacifism remains a greatly attractive option. Violence has not given either Israel or the Palestinians either safety or hope. A mutual restraint might be necessary for both people's survival.

I conclude with profound words from the most prominent Jewish philosopher of the late twentieth century, who died at its end, Emmanuel Levinas:

> I will set out from being in the verbal sense of the word, in which being is suggested and understood, in a sense, as a process of being, an event of being, an adventure of being. A remarkable adventure! The event of being is in a concern with being; it would appear to be its only way of being, in its *élan* which is "essentially" finite and completely absorbed in this concern with being. In a sense, the only thing at issue for the event of being is the being of that very being. To be as such is, from the first, to be preoccupied with being, as if some relaxation were already necessary, some

"tranquilizer," in order to remain – while being – unconcerned about being. To be: already an insistence on being as if a "survival instinct" that coincided with its development, preserving it, and maintaining it in its adventure of being, were its meaning. The tensing of being back onto itself, a plot in which the reflexive pronoun, - self, is bound up. An insistence before all light and decision, the secret of a savagery excluding deliberation and calculation, violence in the guise of beings who affirm themselves "without regard" for one another in their concern to be.

Origin of all violence, varying with the various modes of being: the life of the living, the existence of human beings, the reality of things. The life of the living in the struggle for life; the natural history of human beings in the blood and tears of wars between individuals, nations, and classes; the matter of things, hard matter; solidity; the closed-in-self, all the way down to the level of the subatomic particles of which physicists speak.

But behold! The emergence, in the life lived by the human being (and it is here that the human, as such, begins – pure eventuality, but from the start an eventuality that is pure and holy), of the devoting-of-oneself-to-the-other. In the general economy of being in its inflection back upon itself, a preoccupation with the other, even to the point of sacrifice, even to the possibility of dying for him or her; a responsibility for the other. Otherwise than being! It is this shattering of indifference—even if indifference is statistically dominant—this possibility of one-for-the-other, that constitutes the ethical event. When human existence interrupts and goes beyond its effort to be—its Spinozan *conatus essendi*—there is a vocation of an existing-for-the-other stronger than the threat of death: the fellow human being's existential adventure matters to the *I* more than its own, posing from the start the *I* as responsible for the being of the other; responsible, that is, unique and elect, as an *I* who no longer is just any individual member of the human race. It is as if the emergence of the human in the economy of being upset the meaning and plot and philosophical rank of ontology: the in-itself of being-persisting-in-being goes beyond itself in the gratuitousness of the outside-of-itself-for-the-other, in sacrifice, or the possibility of sacrifice, in the perspective of holiness. [Levinas, p. XIII.]

Bibliography

David Bleich : "Preemptive War in Jewish Law" (*Tradition* 17, 1983)

Gerald Blikstein: *Political Concepts of Maimonides, Halakha*h, Ramat Gan, 2001.

Martin Buber: *Malhut Shamayim*, Jerusalem, 1965 [Kingship of God (New York, 1967)]

Arthur A. Goren, *Dissenter In Zion* ,Cambridge, MA, 1982.

Reuven Kimelman: "Judaism, War and Weapons of Mass Destruction," *Conservative Judaism* 56.1, 2003.

Daniel Landes (ed.), *Confronting Omnicide,* Northvale, 1991.

Emmanuel Levinas, *Entre Nous*, trans. Smith and Harshav, New York, 1998.

Millard C. Lind, *Yahweh Is a Warrior,* Scottsdale, PA, 1980.

Maimonides, *Kings and War*, trans. A.M. Hershman, New Haven, CT, 1963.

George Foot Moore, *Judaism* II, Cambridge, MA, 1944.

Susan Niditch, *War in the Hebrew Bible*, New York, 1993.

H.D. Preuss, "Milhama," Botterweck *et al. Theological Dictionary of the Old Testament,* Grand Rapids, 1997.

David Saperstein, *Preventing the Nuclear Holocaust,* New York, 1983.

Sifre to Numbers, Chapter 42, trans. Neusner, Atlanta, 1986.

Steven Schwarzschild: "Shalom," in *Confrontation* (Long Island University) (Winter, 1981)

Steven Schwarzschild, "The Religious Demand for Peace," *Judaism, Vol.* 15, 1966.

"Ahavat Shalom," Talmudic Encyclopedia, 8:50ff., Jerusalem, 1957.

FIGHTING IN NATIONAL ARMIES

Walter Jacob

In May of 1789, the first Jewish military recruits for the Hapsburg army, under Emperor Joseph II, assembled in Prague were greeted by the following words: "Earn the thanks and honor of the nation; let it be seen that our (Jewish) people, thus far oppressed, love their Lord and are ready, if necessary to sacrifice their lives.... I hope that the loyal service, which you will surely give, will result in the elimination of those half oppressive measures which still restrict us. How much honor and fame will you then receive from all men who seek righteousness and all your fellow citizens. In this spirit I want to give you my heartfelt blessings." These enthusiastic words were spoken by no less than Ezekiel Landau (1713–1793, the chief rabbi of Prague.[1] Why did this careful, middle aged, Orthodox halakhic scholar greet these young recruits with such approval while outside the crowd of relatives was in tears? Did he have any reservations about young Jews serving in a foreign military force, perhaps expressed in a responsum? How did this scholar justify Jewish military service in a war which was neither "obligatory" nor a "permissive" as defined in the rabbinic literature ? Was there any precedent of military service for other nations?

Actually, such warm greetings toward military service accompanied young Jews about to enter military service in all the western European wars in the last two centuries. Patriotic fervor sent young men to fight in the Napoleonic wars, the Prussian War Liberation, the Franco-Prussian War of 1870 and at an even higher pitch on both sides in World War I. Of course this was not so for those impressed for decades into the armies of the Russian Czars.

Subsequently Jews have taken military service for our respective nations for granted. My grandfather, Benno Jacob, served for a year in the Prussian army in 1881 along with tens of thousands of other German Jews. Later during World War I as a rabbi my grandfather visited German troops in France, only a short journey from his Dortmund congregation. I served voluntarily as a military chaplain in the United States Air Force stationed in the Philippines in the next century and traveled thousands of miles each month to far flung bases on the Asian rim of the Pacific Ocean. Neither one of us or the millions of other Jews who served their respective countries ever questioned the nature of this service. Patriotism had quietly replaced any philosophical or halakhic considerations. Were we simply caught up in the nationalistic fervor of the last two centuries?

As Jews we had no honored fighting tradition, no military heroes, and most had never handled a weapon. Hunting had no appeal. Suddenly we became soldiers and accepted the honors which came with soldiering. This happened unexpectedly as so much else in the process of Emancipation. However, why did this occur without the slightest religious discussion or basis in the halakhic tradition. Warfare and soldiering had long ago been relegated to the periphery of our religious concerns. The great codifications of Jewish law hardly mention it.[2]

Only the creation of the State of Israel brought a change. Military service was essential for the existence of the new state and wars followed in rapid succession. The Orthodox community approached this most reluctantly. It sought and received general exemptions from military service for its young men - a source of much bitterness in Israel which has only been corrected in a very limited way.[3] The underlying religious questions about warfare have not been settled. The studies and guides for the Israeli soldier deal with the religious issues for military personnel in the Israeli forces and in the various Israeli wars. They do not deal with Jewish military service in the diaspora armies.[4]

These Israeli issues will not be discussed in this paper. It limits itself to a Jewish understanding of Jewish military service in the modern nation states in which most Jews live. Jews have accepted their responsibility as soldiers along with every one else willingly and often with enthusiasm. As the practical and theological path of Judaism has always found expression through the halakhah. What does the halakhah say about soldiering in national armies and modern national warfare. How has this been incorporated into our modern Jewish religious views. Does this represent a radical departure from an age old tradition or is it simply an adaptation to new circumstances?

Our nineteenth century emancipation, however slow, was welcomed and hailed by every Jewish community. The Jewish condition of an oppressed, semi-autonomous community was slowly replaced by citizenship in the lands in which we lived. It was welcomed, but along with it came fundamental changes in every aspect of our life as Jews. We were happy with the freedom and new status and sought to make adjustments as a religious community operating within the limits now placed by the nation state. The all encompassing Judaism with its broad jurisdiction over a total way of life was surrendered. Discussions of matters formerly within the religious purview were abandoned whether out of fear of the national authorities or in deference to the communal desire for the new freedom. The traditional community built fences around what was left; its rabbinic leadership focused on synagogue ritual rather than fundamentals. The Reform community sought to change the traditions to accommodate the new situation and then to redefine Judaism. Questions of a more basic nature were left undiscussed. Among them were the relationship with the nation state and its limits over the lives of its citizens. This included military service as well as pacifism, and a good deal else.[5]

We need to place the issue of military service into a historical framework. How did the Jewish attitudes toward warfare develop through the centuries. There were radical changes as well as long quiet periods and we should be aware of them.

THE BIBLICAL PAST

Our biblical past presents a record of endless wars and conflict;[6] it is the history of a small embattled nation, not too different from that of modern Israel more or less constant strife. Ecclesiastes - "a time for war and a time for peace" (3:8) is appropriate with its emphasis on war. God is depicted as warrior in the Song at the Sea (Ex 15.3) and warlike (Ex 17:16, Jud 5:13; Ps 24.:8;) with the holy ark of the covenant accompanying the troops into battle (I Sam 4:4; II Sam 11:11 ff.) in the earlytimes. However God also destroyed the instruments of war (Ps 76.4; Hos 1:7; 2:20) and brought an end to war (Is 2:4). Yet, the books of Joshua, Judges, I and II Kings, I and II Chronicles record centuries of virtually continuous warfare. This pattern continued through the period of the Maccabees and Herod until it ended under Roman domination. The Jewish armies were provided with some legislative guidance which dealt with many details including who should be excused from fighting, treatment of the enemy forces and non-combatants, sieges, etc.[7] Much of this was ignored in actual combat. The wars themselves were often denounced by the prophets along with the cruelty and suffering which they brought to all.

The limited legislation governing combat was not discussed or expanded in the historical account or in the prophetic books. For example, there was no discussion of the idealistic legislation of Deuteronomy which permitted exemption from military service for those who had built a new house and not yet enjoyed it, planted a vineyard and not yet harvested it, become engaged, but not yet married, and anyone who is afraid (Deut 20:5 ff.). There are discussions of female captives whom a soldier wished to marry (Deut 21:10), and of the destruction which could take place during a siege (Deut 20:10 ff.). War along with the treatment of the enemy was harsh, often cruel, and the reports contained only the facts without moral comment (Ex 17:9; Deut 7.16 ff; Josh 8:24 ff.; Josh 10.28 ff; Jud 3:29; I Sam 27:9; I Sam 15:13 ff; I Sam. 10:6 ff.; etc.). King Asa, contrary to Deuteronomy, permitted "no exemptions" from military service (I K 15.22). Mighty warriors were glorified at some length (I Chron 11:22 ff.); detailed accounts of the army were given (I Chron 12:24 ff.; II Chron. 1:14 ff.); and warfare was taken for granted without comment (II Chron 13:2 ff.; 14:7; 17:12 ff.). The slaughter, taking of captives, and ransacking was simply recorded without comment (II Chron 28:6 ff). God was seen as a fighter (II Chron 32:21) also earlier in the Song at the Sea (Ex 15:3 ff.). These, especially in the Books of Chronicles, are historical records with an implied theology which glorified warfare.

Military service was taken for granted and the horrors of war were disguised as a necessity of what we would euphemistically call "nation building." The ideal of a peaceful world was proclaimed by the prophets as a distant dream of the Messianic Age (Jer 65:25; Micah 4:3; Is. 2:4); they also spoke out against all violence (Is. 60.18; Jer. 23.3; Ezek. 45.9). We should remember that some of the prophets, who were part of the royal court, usually supported the war about to be fought (I K 22.6 ff., etc.) though not always as we hear from the prophet Jehu (I K 16.7). The biblical tradition did not preserve their messages.

THE SECOND COMMONWEALTH

The wars of the Maccabees were national struggle for survival with the forces of a mighty empire. National and religious emotions combined to make this a bitter struggle, eventually won at a huge cost. The religious group responsible for the war adopted a policy which permitted both defensive and offensive fighting on *shabbat*.[8] Nothing about this was mentioned anywhere in the Bible and it is unlikely that the armies of the Israelite and Judean kings rested on the sabbath. We know nothing about the development of the detailed *shabbat* laws. The tradition prohibiting fighting developed in centuries when Jews were no longer engaged in warfare.

From the time of the Maccabees (165 B.C.E.) through the rule of Herod (37 B.C.E.– 4 C.E.) to the end of the revolt of Bar Kochba (135 C.E.), the Land of Israel was subjected to almost continuous warfare. The record of these struggles has mainly been preserved in the Books of Maccabees and the historical writings of Flavius Josephus. The fighting was savage and the cruelties were recorded without comment.[9] By this time large Jewish communities, possibly the majority of the Jewish population, lived outside the Land of Israel in Egypt, Mesopotamia, and the Roman Empire.

Later reports of the revolts against Roman rule in 68–73 C.E. and 132 C.E. were very limited in the traditional Jewish literature. The entire period was glossed over or suppressed as the Jewish leadership wished to stop further revolts with their tremendous loss of lives. There was no further development even of theories of warfare. The subject was generally ignored as it seemed irrelevant. The sole Jewish involvement in warfare was among the legendary Chazar kingdom (ca. 900 C.E. , about which we know very little.[10]

MISHNAH, TALMUD, RABBINIC PERIOD

The changed view, forced upon us and then adopted after the bloody defeats inflicted by the Romans, led to the abandonment of this topic. The rabbinic leadership moved in a different direction after the two disastrous national defeats inflicted by the Roman super-power in 70 and 135 C.E. The rabbis suppressed the militant history of the Maccabees and emphasized an innocent miracle for the popular holiday of Hannukah while Judah Maccabee disappeared into a vague haze. Through *midrashim* biblical military heroes like David became principally a psalmist and so were transformed into literary figures. Many warriors were transfigured into rabbinic scholars like themselves – Moses became *moshe rabenu;*[11] this effort became very clear as a long line of biblical figures reappear in the rabbinic literature.

Talmudic scholars, far removed from the realities of war, then created a military theory which divided wars into two categories – "mandatory" (*Milhemet mitzvah*) and "discretionary" (*milhemet reshut*). These discussions are mainly found in *Mishnah* Sotah 8 and the later talmudic discussions in Sotah 43 b and 44 a,b as well as parallel statements in the *Sifre*. A section in Hor. 12 a,b further described the role of the high priest while making the declaration of Deut 20:3-5.[12] All of this really centered around the divine command to conquer the land of Israel which had been promised to Abraham and his descendants. Conquering the land of Israel was a mandated war and therefore obligatory, while the wars of David and later kings which expanded the territory were not. Never mind that they were often conducted in areas which could be included in the vague original divine promise and its later interpretations.[13]

The exemptions from military service mentioned in Deuteronomy were understood to apply only to the latter kind of warfare. A further discussion of "discretionary war" is found in San 20a (*Mishnah* San. 2a) which demanded that such wars needed the permission of the Great Sanhedrin composed of seventy-one members or perhaps could be simply undertaken by the king. The matter became further complicated by the discussion in Sanhedrin 16a and Berakhot 3b which stated that the king must also seek the advice of the *urim vetumin* - in other words divine approval given through the priests. These conditions made a "discretionary war" not even theoretically possible. Additional discussions of warfare appeared in concerns about defensive actions on *shabbat*. They were permitted even if initially the attackers only wished to haul off some hay. On the same page there is a brief discussion of transgressing the *eruv* in order to retrieve weapons needed for self defense. (Eruvin 45a). Building fortifications around a city or otherwise securing its defenses against future attack was discussed, including the levying of taxes for this purpose (B.B. 7b, 8a).

Considering the bulk of the Talmud, the limited discussion on these few pages demonstrates the scant halakhic interest in war during these centuries. No tractate of the Talmud or major section of this vast work dealt with either a theory of warfare or with the efforts to limit its effect on combatants and the bi-standers who have always been the main sufferers. There was no desire to elaborate on the biblical texts or to develop a full theological approach to warfare and all the problems which it brought.

The talmudic material was presented in a tightly organized form by Maimonides (1135–1204).[14] He summarized that the conquest of the Land of Israel and its national defense was a mandated war and therefore obligatory upon the citizenry while the wars of the kings of Israel and Judea needed the approval of the Sanhedrin, the "Great Assembly." For the former, war provisions, land for roads or fortifications could be requisitioned without recourse by the citizenry and the citizens were obligated to fight. Only in the latter type of war, the "discretionary" struggles could the laws of Deuteronomy about individual deferral from military service be invoked. These pseudo-military decisions based upon discussions carried out in rabbinic academies through the centuries were, of course, purely theoretical and peripheral to the major concerns of these sages. They were based on vague scriptural citations which had never been fully developed into a theory of warfare and its ethical implications.

When we look to Jewish philosophical writings from Philo (ca. 40) through Saadiah (882–942) to the twentieth century, we find only the most incidental discussion of war. Levi ben Gerson's (Gersonides 1288–1344) *Milhamot Adonai* (*Wars of God*) has a misleading title, from our perspective, as it did not deal with war.

Many later Jewish halakhic scholars, such as Asher ben Jechiel (1250–1327), Jacob ben Asher (1269–1343), and Joseph Karo (1488–1575), who systematized Jewish legislation from the Bible to their time, almost entirely ignored military legislation as it had no practical purpose outside a sovereign Jewish state. Only Maimonides who wished to provide a system which could also serve a future Jewish state, not only organized the laws of warfare, but also developed them further. Maimonides' summary expanded the talmudic texts in a number of ways: First by virtue of placing everything together and into an organized context. Secondly he made decisions on matters over which the earlier authorities disagreed and finally by developing the entire matter into a system. The casual remarks of talmudic scholars, usually not debated were placed into a setting in which the power of the king was severely circumscribed. We should note a contrast to the expansion of royal emergency powers.[15] Retaking the Land of Israel remained an obligation; wars of expansion were placed in a gray area, while other wars were subject to the vote of the "Great Assembly," which could theoretically be recreated As the borders of the Land of Israel were subject to enormous variations of interpretation, those restrictions were limited. Furthermore few of the details of warfare were touched upon by these broad brush-strokes. If we look at the totality of the *Mishneh Torah*, this section did not loom large. In the subsequent halakhic and philosophical literature no efforts were made to provide a theoretical framework for war.

JEWISH SOLDIERS IN THE DIASPORA

Jacob ben Asher (1269–1343) was among the first to discuss or mention military service of Jewish soldiers in the Diaspora; with the statement that: "A Jew may participate in a permissive war if it began three days before *shabbat*..., but in a mandatory war, even on *shabbat*,"[16] He based himself on a brief talmudic comment (Shab. 19a). A mandatory struggle would include Jewish participation in the defense of a city along with the other inhabitants. The principle that "danger to life" over-rides all *shabbat* prohibitions was cited in defense of this decision.

The nature of such a struggle between gentiles in which Jews participated along with everyone else was never raised. Joseph Karo's (1488–1575) commentary on this passage stated that there was no need for Jews to participate in such a struggle between gentile forces. However, Joel Sirkes (1561–1640) countered that Jews had a responsibility to participate. He disagreed with Karo's decision and in his rejoinder emphasized that Karo had "forgotten that Jews fought to protect their cities along with Gentiles ... furthermore it was an obligatory struggle when it was conducted to aid fellow Jews."[17] Jewish participation in such militias created to face a temporary crisis alongside more permanent military units seems to have been common. We need to remember that this was not a major discussion, but a brief set of comments on sabbath laws, much shorter than all other matters connected with *shabbat*.

JEWISH MERCENARIES AND DEFENSE UNITS

The realities of Jewish life and the halakhah parted company, at least to some extent here as in many other areas. Jewish mercenaries as individuals fought in armies through the millennia, but were either forgotten or ignored. An exception was the Jewish mercenary unit which served in Egypt as a garrison (600 B.C.E.), before the Persian conquest, and later under the Ptolemaic rulers of Egypt on the island of Elephantine in the upper Nile (300 B.C.E.). This was mentioned in *Letters to Aristeas*[18] and further illuminated through papyri discovered in 1906–1908. The latter produced interesting religious, economic, and personal information about these soldiers, and the community, but little about their military service, organization, or the rationale for this type of "foreign legion."[19]

More important was the participation in local militias during times of crisis. Towns and cities were frequently besieged and none had a standing army large enough to defend themselves. In times of peace the military was intended to maintain local order and take care of brigands in the neighborhood. It had to be be sufficiently large to protect against local uprisings, and impress jealous neighbors that any attack would be costly and difficult. These forces were not sufficient to defend against a major army set on conquest. As military costs have always been high, few could afford a large army in constant readiness for any eventuality. Militias of the citizenry was the only alternative. Due to the disruption of normal life and the reluctance of the inhabitants it could not be called out till the enemy was virtually outside the walls. Jews participated as reluctantly, as everyone else.

As some Jews were engaged in trade, which carried them further afield, they were perhaps better informed about potentially hostile neighbors.

Jews were included in such militias despite anti-Semitic feelings as seen in the discussion by Karo and Sirkes mentioned earlier. Although the number of Jews in any community was small, every person counted and every able bodied man was needed. Their participation did not lead to better relations in peaceful times. We should note that the Jewish community were usually too small to undertake successful self-defense during riots by the local population. Jews fighting to defend a city were taken for granted by the rabbinic authorities without any halakhic discussion. Presumably Jews fought on *shabbat* when needed along with everyone else. Such defensive engagements in contrast to the adventures of ambitious monarchs were accepted without discussion. We know that in Spain Jews joined local militia in defense of their towns and occasionally also served in royal armies.[20] Alfonso VI in 1086 even proposed that the battle of Sacralias-Zallaka be postponed from Friday to Monday so that the holy days of Muslims, Christians, and Jews would not interfere.[21]

A few Jews were involved in battle; among them was Samuel Ha-Nagid (993–1056) who is said to have written some of his beautiful poetry on the battlefield, but we do not know whether he actually fought.[22] During the period of the Crusades, Jews defended themselves by donning "their armor and girding on their weapons, and at their head was Rabbi Kalonymous ben Meshullam."[23] At about the same time the Messianic pretender, David Alroy, appealed to the Jews of Persia for assistance in an armed uprising which was to conquer Jerusalem.[24]

During the Crusades some Jews went further and organized units to defend their community against the Crusaders. As those armies marched through the Rhineland, they attacked the Jewish communities as well as the towns in which they lived. The Christian neighbors often also fought to defend them, but usually in vain. When the besiegers left, the military service ceased, for those who survived.[25]

Through the Middle Ages we hear echoes of individual Jewish soldiers who served in various military units usually in the discussion of different matters and often directly in responsa. Meir of Rothenburg (1215–1293) stated that it was forbidden to enter a synagogue with swords, which were worn by Christian physicians decoratively as a sign of their status; yet Mahari Weil (died 1455) stated that those who do so will not go to paradise; other studies like the *Rokeah* permitted swords.[26]

Much later, a responsum of Meir of Lublin (1558–1616) dealt with an accidental shooting during musket practice as the Jews were learning to defend the community against the Tartar invasion.[27] These glimpses of individuals are picturesque and make interesting reading, but had no influence on Jewish life. In Prague such service was recognized, so Ferdinand I in 1523 enlisted Jews in the defense of Eisenstadt and Ferdinand II (1619–1637) praised the community for their help in defending Prague against the Swedish army. Later Charles IV rewarded the Jewish community of Prague with the famous flag placed in the Altneuschul. We should note that the privilege of bearing arms permanently was not granted anywhere.

The Jewish population was often taxed for the military adventures of the rulers. These imposts could be extraordinarily high, but were the only way to procure the right of settlement. We should also note that many of the wealthiest Jews of the Middle Ages made their fortunes through supplying the military forces of the rulers, at times even recruiting them, and always lending the funds for those wars. Such ventures were extremely risky and Christian bankers avoided them. The Jewish bankers depended on such income to survive and frequently lost their position along with their wealth, both when the ruler was successful in his military ambitions and when he failed or was slain.[28] Among the best known of such Court Jews in a slightly later period were Samuel Oppenheimer (1635–1703) and Samson Wertheimer (1658–1724). This continued still later with individuals such as Michael Gratz who was a blockade runner during the American Revolution. However Jews were not personally involved in these military ventures.

Other references in the Middle Ages deal with armed Jewish merchants who set out in groups and partially armed for self protection when they traveled to fairs or on other business ventures. As nation states did not exist and as principalities rarely possessed the power to patrol even their own domain adequately, brigandry was rife and the roads were dangerous. This, however, could not be considered as military service.

LATE MIDDLE AGES AND MODERN TIMES

The role of Jews in military matters was limited even when the nature of warfare changed through the use of firearms. This ended the feudal era's dominance of knights as a soldier equipped with relatively cheap weaponry could overcome the heavily armed mounted knight. In the new armies, commissions continued to go to the nobility who frequently recruited and equipped their own forces. Common soldiers and ancillary forces were recruited from the lower nobility and the poorer classes for whom it represented upward mobility, a way out of the grinding poverty, as well as a source of adventure. In some instances cash bounties were also involved. As many wars were religious or ethnic, military forces were composed of co-religionists or of the same ethnic group. Mercenary units played an important role in all wars. We may remember that the British hired Hessian units to fight the American revolutionaries. Such units were justifiably feared as they often raped, looted, and pillaged.[29] An occasional Jew served in similar European units, because of special skills in metallurgy, other technical matters or the knowledge of foreign languages. All this preceded the creation of nation states with their hunger for manpower for their much larger armies.

TOWARD EMANCIPATION

An early sign of a new dawn was provided in New Amsterdam where two Jews tried to enrole in the militia as they were unwilling to pay a tax imposed on Jews for an unwanted exemption. Asser Levy forced the issue upon Governor Stuyvesant, who turned to the East India Company in Holland for a resolution, and so in 1655 he was accepted.[30]

Joseph II of Austria who wanted to make the Jewish minority more useful to the country, issued an "Edict of Toleration" (1782) which removed some restrictions and was followed by an edict (1788) which mandated military service for Jews, but without extending full citizenship. All this came after the cruel repressive measures of his mother Maria Teresa (1744) which expelled Jews from vast areas of her empire in mid-winter. Although the Jewish community welcomed Joseph II's step toward rights, they hated the conscription. When twenty-five Jewish recruits were assembled in Prague, the Jewish community went into mourning. Yet Ezekiel Landau encouraged them with the words with which this paper began even though military service was for a period of seven years. Many Jews saw this as a step toward emancipation. Others understood it as an additional burden and destructive. It placed Jews into a non-Jewish setting, led to the desecration of the *shabbat*, the consumption of forbidden foods, etc.

The leaders of the Jewish community appealed to remove compulsory military service, but failed except for a short period in some provinces. Even there compulsory service was re-introduced in 1804. Communities declared days of mourning when Jews were drafted into the army.

JEWISH SOLDIERS IN THE NEW NATIONAL ARMIES

The mass levees for the large armies of the French Revolution and subsequently napoleonic wars raised the number of Jews serving in national military armies. This began with the "War of the First Coalition" (1792 –1793) which sought to spread the revolution to the rest of Europe. All unmarried men between 18 and 25 were called to arms and so an army of half a million men was raised quickly. As the Jewish population of France was negligible, few Jews were involved. Soon, however, Napoleon expanded these forced call-ups into the newly liberated lands, so that his Grand Army of 1812 consisting of 611,000 soldiers of whom only 230,000 were French. A greater number of Jews were involved; many adopted new names in order to conceal their Jewish identity for fear of anti-Semitism.[31] Therefore the number of Jews who served remains unknown. Jews, although not full citizens, were forced to participate. Some along with many non-Jews emigrated to the New World to escape military service, as later from Tsarist Russia.

An entirely different situation arose with the "War of Liberation" fought by Prussia (1813 –1814). More than five hundred Jews volunteered for military service.[32] Many distinguished themselves. Enthusiastic Jewish soldiers participated also and in the wars of liberation and unification soon fought in Italy and Hungary. Some Jews distinguished themselves as leaders and their service was fully recognized. This completely voluntary military service presented a a new phenomenon. In 1866 eleven hundred Jewish soldiers fought in the Prussian army and fourteen thousand in the Franco-Prussian War of 1870. The Austrian army enrolled an even larger number of Jews with thirty thousand by 1870, among them were two hundred officers.

Rabbis petitioned their respective German governments for furloughs during the High Holidays and other accommodations in the mid-nineteenth centurywith some success.[33] Jews served in the military units of various German states and gained commissions as officers in Bavaria, but not in Prussia.[34] That the struggle for this right became a cause celebre demonstrated the height of military fervor in the Jewish community. No real change came about till World War I and even then anti-Semitism limited such commissions. The War Ministry did, however, make other practical concessions for Jewish soldiers by providing ritual wine and flour for *matzot* during World War I.

When Germany and her allies lost the war, anti-Semitic charges of Jewish soldiers malingering sought to make Jewish soldiers scape-goats for the German defeat. The ninety-six thousand Jews veterans among whom thirty-thousand had been decorated for valor organized themselves and bitterly denounced these accusations. They did not give up and published a volume commemorating more than twelve thousand German Jews who had lost their lives in World War I even at the beginning of the Nazi period.[35]

In the twenty-first century the German army has published a number of booklets which reviews the service of Jewish soldiers in the past. It mandates that Jewish religious observances are recognized. An organization of Jewish soldiers was founded in 2006.[36]

Developments in Austria were somewhat different. The Habsburg Empire's military command had been reluctant to have Jews in the army, but the 1788 Edict of Joseph II forced the issue. This army proved to be more accommodating than any other as it had to deal with a large number of minorities.; when possible it permitted Jewish soldiers to mess together. By the middle of the nineteenth century various efforts to overcome *shabbat* and dietary problems met with some success. The fact that some Jews served in the Hungarian revolutionary armies did not change this. Jews rose in the ranks with a high percentage of officers. By 1866 provisions had been made for Jewish chaplains. Although the army was restricted to 30,000 soldiers after World War I, Jews continued to serve without prejudice until the Nazi take-over in 1938.[37]

In some other European countries Jews who sought officer status were also able to gain it despite anti-Semitism. The most serious anti-Semitic charges were those which led to the Dreyfus Affair in France (1899–1914). It became a major political issue which involved the entire French society. We should not forget the a small number of Jews who enlisted in the French Foreign Legion, a force mainly created to deal with unrest in the French colonies scattered around the world.[38]

In the United States Jewish soldiers fought in the Revolution and all later wars either as volunteers and beginning with the Civil War as draftees. The rise of anti-Semitism at the end of the nineteenth century prompted Simon Wolf to present a summary of Jewish military service in all wars mentioning specific individuals as well as those who received the Congressional Medal of Honor. However, the main task which he set for himself was a complete list of Jewish soldiers in the Union Armies of the Civil War.[39] Numerous articles and booklets on the Jewish participation in later wars have also appeared.

RUSSIAN MANDATORY SERVICE

Matters were very different in Russia especially after Nicholas I ascended the throne in 1825. Jews, along with the merchant class, had been excused from military service through the payment of an additional tax. In 1827 an Ukase demanded the military service of ten recruits per thousand between the ages of twelve and twenty-five; this was more than the seven per thousand asked of the general population. Often that number was further increased. This was part of the Tsar's effort to destroy the Jewish identity of the very young conscripts; it was never connected with promises of citizenship.

All efforts including bribery to change this decree, failed. Guild merchants, artisans, rabbis, and farmers were excused. Many children of poor Russian Jews tried to emigrate; some maimed themselves. When not enough Jewish youth could be found, lads from twelve to eighteen were taken off the street into military service; sometimes children as young as six were included. These children were placed in "cantonist" schools often in Siberia, hundreds of miles away, in an effort to convert them. The traveler and journalist, Alexander Herzen (1835) reported their plight as they stood half frozen, bullied by older soldiers, thousands of miles from home. A third of the group which he met in a distant Siberian village had not survived the journey and many more died later.[40]

Each Jewish community was considered as a separate unit and was responsible for its quota of recruits; individuals could purchase a substitute, but only among fellow Jews. The oath forced upon the soldiers demanded faithful service and a break with their past. Forbidden to observe anything Jewish, forced to eat pork, many were forcibly converted and life generally became miserable. This was part of a larger Czarist plan to force conversion to Christianity. Cantonist were also excluded from the rank of officers.[41] This system was existed from 1827 to 1856, to be replaced by another, only slightly better. Between 1874 and 1892, 173,434 Jews served in the Russian army. Despite this terrible treatment, Jews also served with distinction even in the Russo-Japanese War (1904) in the face of simultaneous pogroms in European Russia. No relief from this tragic episode in Jewish life was possible except emigration, mainly to North America, but also to European and other lands. Yet more than half a million Jewish soldiers served the Czar in World War I.

The Halakhah and Mandatory Military Service

Military service had to be accepted and the rabbinic and communal leadership could only try to place it into the framework of the halakhah. None of the responsa discussed the question of fighting in the armies of a non-Jewish state. There was no halakhic precedent for the stringent conditions which had to be faced The questions addressed to the rabbis dealt with the problems of observance for Jewish soldiers in the army, such as *shabbat*, dietary laws, etc. As military life had become a norm, how could the Jewish communities help the Jewish recruits and their families? Although similar questions faced Jewish soldiers elsewhere, Russian mandatory military service, which lasted for decades with its conversionist goal, presented different issues.[42]

The obligation of filling the quota of recruits which had been placed upon the Jewish communities remained a contentious issue. Communal leaders sought to substitute the payment of a fine, but the government rejected this concept. The rabbinic authorities were forced to understand this as *dina demalkhuta dina* and tried to set some guidelines. The first issue raised was the possibility of hiring substitutes as, naturally, each young man tried to free himself from the obligation. Some suggested that trouble makers among the young people be singled out and conscripted, however, Ezekiel Landau (1713–1793) rabbi in Prague, who dealt with this issue in Austria and strongly rejected this. [43]

Another way out was through the purchase of a substitute, another Jew who was willing to serve for an appropriate payment. Was it permissible to place the life of another person at risk even if that person was willing ? Landau, dealt with this as well and rejected it by citing the well known example of a besieger of a town who demanded that a specific Jew be delivered, otherwise all Jews would be killed. Landau indicated that the request could be met as it was for a specific person and the that person, could be surrendered. However, purchasing the service of a poorer Jew as a substitute was not a parallel example. [44] Not everyone agreed, so Meir Esh, a Hungarian pupil of Hatam Sofer, argued that those who were willing to serve as substitutes understood the danger. They also knew that military service entailed violating many commandments, but did not mind. Thus they were already liable for divine punishment. Furthermore military service although potentially dangerous, was not absolutely dangerous in times of peace, therefore the purchase of a substitute was permissible.[45]

Moses Schreiber (Hatam Sofer 1762–1839) reacted to conscription by trying to free a number of boys from such service, but without success. In a responsum he concluded that some form of purchasing out, if it did not involve another individual, was permitted though under the government rules unlikely. Military service was mandatory under the rubric of *dina d'malkhuta dina*; the obligation rested upon each individual and so should be solved individually and not by the community as a whole. The Gentile ruler who had ultimate power had to be obeyed. Hatam Sofer suggested that God used such rulers to punish the Jewish people for their misdeeds. He, however, continued by stating that some rabbinic authorities tried to limit a ruler's jurisdiction to "legitimate demands." Therefore outrageous financial imposts could be opposed and circumvented in any way (citing Solomon B. Adret and Meir Rothenburg). Sofer, however, considered military service as legitimate urged that it be accepted. He along with others suggested that a system of lots represented a fair way to solve the problem for the communal leaders who were responsible for the quota.[46] The German scholars, David Hoffman (1843–1921) also felt that such service was the obligation of all citizens and went further by stating that individuals should not seek even a temporary deferment or non military service.[47]

The question of payment to the government in lieu of military service continued to be pursued. Some local authorities were willing to accept it. This raised the issue whether communal funds could be used as such payment could be seen as akin to the redemption of captives; traditionally that took precedence over any other use of *tzedakah* funds.[48] Hiring a substitute which seems to have been common in Russia was acceptable to Meir Eisenstadt as stated in his *Imrei Esh*.[49] However there was general agreement that after a person had been drafted, he was not permitted to seek a substitute.[50] Once in the army, the recruit was obliged to obey all commands even if given on *shabbat*. By World War I rabbinic authorities such as Moses Samuel Glassner of Klosenburg argued sharply that every conscript had to serve and any attempt to escape the obligation was immoral. Israel Meir Hakohen (*Hofetz Hayyim*) considered it sinful to evade military service.[51] Military service should no longer be seen as *dina demalhuta dina*, i.e. as forced, but as a sacred obligation of citizenship.[52] Eliezer Waldenberg (1915–2006) much later stated that it was permissible to volunteer for military service despite the knowledge that many Jewish commandments could not be obeyed.[53]

A much broader concern was raised by Zeev Leiter. He understood that Jews were now recruited into all national armies and therefore Jews would be fighting fellow Jews. With this in mind should Jews willingly serve in any army?[54]

Despite these caveats military service was accepted and the responsa turned to specific issues connected with such service. There was little use in discussing the obligations of daily prayer, *minyan, shabbat* observance, dietary laws, etc. and they were left to the individual to do what was possible. *Dina demalkhuta dina* and escaping danger to one's life were frequent rationales cited by both sides in this debate.

The private issues were left to the individual, but the broader communal issues could not be escaped. When a Jewish soldier was killed, if married, his wife could well become an *agunah* as witnesses normally considered competent did not exist or there were none. This presented a series of family issues which involved the entire community with the potential of a large number of women left as *agunot* along with the economic issues which needed to be resolved.

Death without witnesses has always been a problem, but it was rare; now it could affect thousands. Was the official testimony of the state acceptable? Could now nonobservant Jewish soldiers testify? Would soldiers who violated *shabbat* and dietary laws be considered "kosher" witnesses? Contradictory responses appeared to these and similar questions. Joseph Saul Nathanson (1810–1875), for example, considered such violators as acting under duress; they had been law abiding and so their testimony was valid. [55] On the other hand Akiba Eger (1761–1837) suspected their veracity even if understood as serving under duress.[56] Mordecai Benet (1753–1829) agreed and considered such witnesses *posul* from Torah.[57] Meir Esh of Hungary rejected such testimony on the grounds that these individuals would not return to the path of the Torah after military service and always rejected such testimony.[58] While Hayyim of Zanz accepted such testimony unless there was convincing evidence that the soldiers were actually *pasul*. Their statements should not be rejected just because they were soldiers, but only if someone testified against their status.[59] Judah Assad (1797–1866) felt that as we accept the statement of women, so we can accept the statement of such Jewish soldiers.[60]

Hayyim Judah Leb of Brody distinguished between the previous generation and his own. In the earlier generation the members of the community sought to avoid military service and those who joined were not religious; however now that military service was obligatory, individuals were and their testimony was to be accepted.[61] Similarly Abraham Benjamin Sofer (1815–1871) accepted such individuals as witnesses on the reasoning that all had been done at the command of the king, so *dina demalhuta dina* prevailed. Furthermore he indicated that their violation of Jewish precepts had not occurred publicly in the Jewish community or among known fellow Jews, so it was impossible to judge them.[62] Interestingly enough Shlomo Dremer in his *Bet Shelomo* provided a very different reason. He claimed that most Jews in Austria were non-observant with only a small number religious, so we can never accept such testimony. [63] Moshe Schick (1807–1879) stated that the testimony of Jewish soldiers might be invalid, but should not be rejected out of hand.[64] Hayyim Sofer looked at this matter from a theological perspective. He felt that we could accept such testimony when it presents an issue between man and God, but not between man and his fellow human being as that might increase *mamzerim* in Israel .[65] In other words a negative response.

One way out of this dilemma was through a conditional divorce (*get al tenai*); it solved the problem of witnesses to the death, but raised other issues aside from the fact that many women were unwilling to accept such a divorce.

Halitzah, provided another set of problems especially in Russia. Sometimes a woman only belatedly discovered that her husband had a brother, who may have been dragooned into the army as a cantonist. Was she obligated to locate him and persuade him to go through this ritual. He may no longer have been Jewish and, of course, did not know her or the ritual. Furthermore how was this to be done in Siberia far from any Jewish community? In lieu of this, could the testimony of the commanding officer to the death of the cantonist be considered valid, even if it may have simply represented a way out for an unwilling soldier? Various responsa dealt with this issue and the related ramifications. [66]

These and responsa on other issues demonstrate that military service in foreign armies was acknowledged as obligatory by the Orthodox community. The Reform community faced the issues discussed above by accepting the testimony of the state for a soldier's death. If missing, the declaration of death after a suitable period was also considered sufficient to solve issues surrounding his widow.

Many other halakhic issues were raised and a broad range of answers given. Some national armies made an effort to provide properly for the Jewish soldiers, both in religious services and *kashrut*.[67] David Hoffmann (1843–1921) wrote a number of lenient responsa on these matters. Rabbis counseled recruits, who came to them, to quietly observe as much of *kashrut*, and other commandments as possible. Issues surrounding *kohanim* were also treated.[68]

By the middle of the nineteenth century tens of thousands of Jewish soldiers were serving in national armies. National loyalties had become so powerful by the twentieth century that Jews left Palestine in order to fight in the armies of their former home land. There were Jewish heroes even in the Czarist armies. Jews rose in the ranks of many armies for example the Jewish general Monash (1865–1931) commanded the Australian Expeditionary Force.[69]

We should note that no national Jewish community made any effort to provide a common approach to the practical questions surrounding military service by Jewish personnel. Nor were there halakhic discussions about the appropriateness of volunteering for military service. In contrast to the lengthy controversies over the organ in a synagogue, vernacular prayers, the role of women in Jewish life and a host of other matters, compulsory and voluntary military service was quietly and universally accepted as part of full citizenship or even without it. The new pattern of life prevailed and was incorporated into Jewish communal life.

MILITARY CHAPLAINS

Christian clergy accompanied military units long before national armies came into existence. In the nineteenth century when Jews began to serve as soldiers, rabbinic services were usually provided by local rabbis on an informal basis. Soldiers often organized *minyanim* and looked after other needs as well. As many 19th and early 20th century wars were fought close to their home community, local rabbis could be helpful. Although the total number of Jews in an army was substantial, the number in a specific unit was too small to demand a full time rabbi. However by the middle of the nineteenth century the need for rabbinic services began to be felt and efforts were made to appoint part or full time chaplains.

The Austrian Emperor Francis Joseph made provisions for Jewish military chaplains in 1866, some thirty years after Protestant chaplains had been provided in his predominantly Catholic nation. By 1914 ten chaplains with the rank of captain had been appointed; that number grew to fifty-six toward the end of World War I while local rabbis augmented their efforts. Small permanent synagogues were built in the larger installations. The chaplains provided religious services, kosher food, etc. and in some instances also conducted religious services for Russian Jewish prisoners of war. They also censored Hebrew letters. Eventually the Austrian army also provided Muslim chaplains.

It took much longer in Germany as the famous picture of Rosh Hashanah services in the Franco-Prussian War of 1870 showed. That service, attended by hundreds of Jewish soldiers, was led by a civilian rabbi. Requests for Jewish chaplains did not succeed in Germany until the beginning of World War I. In contrast to the Christian chaplains, they received neither military rank, nor payment by the government. That remained an obligation of the Jewish community. In German occupied Poland these Jewish chaplains also aided the civilian population as vividly described by Emanuel Carlebach. They also provided for the religious needs of Russian Jewish prisoners of war.[70] The political split between the Liberal and Orthodox German community limited cooperation and meant that fewer Orthodox chaplains were appointed. A field prayer book was published in Berlin in 1916 and another in Vilna in 1918.[71]

In the American armed forces matters were different. The American Revolutionary army (1775–1781) had Protestant chaplains, independently provided by each unit. This pattern continued in the succeeding wars till the Civil War (1861–1865) when Catholic chaplains were also provided. Jewish soldiers served in each of these wars, but as the Jewish population was small, there were few Jewish soldiers. As each military unit elected its own officers and chaplains, an occasional Jew was also chosen.[72]

As many Jews served as soldiers in the American Civil War, the question of a Jewish chaplain arose. Rev. Arnold Fischel became a volunteer chaplain in the northern army while lobbying with the help of the Jewish community for an official Jewish chaplaincy. In 1862 Rabbi Jacob Frankel became the first of three Jewish military chaplains appointed by President Lincoln.[73] They became an official part of the military establishment.

In World War I the Jewish Welfare Board became the endorsing agency for American Jewish chaplains. In 1917 it published an abridged prayer book under the direction of three rabbis representing the Orthodox, Reform, and Conservative groups. Rabbi Elkan Voorsanger became the first American Jewish chaplain assigned to a combat unit in November of 1917. Twenty-six rabbis served as chaplains in the American army. In World War II the same general pattern prevailed; a new prayer book including a Reform service was published in 1941. Three hundred and eleven Jewish chaplains served in the various branches of the American armed forces and more than 700,000 copies of the military prayer book were distributed. With the beginning of the Korean War the three major rabbinic groups imposed a draft upon themselves to assure a steady supply of military chaplains and this continued to 1966. Jewish military chaplains regularly serve in the American armed forces to the present.[74]Like their Protestant and Catholic counterparts, Jewish chaplains in the American military forces have been trained to serve all soldiers with ethical issues in emergencies with religious matters.

In 1943 the Jewish Welfare Board organized a committee on responsa composed of Leo Jung for the Orthodox community, Milton Steinberg for the Conservative community and Solomon B. Freehof, who became the chairman, for the Reform community. They were to issue responsa on halakhic matters for the armed forces and did so throughout World War II. This represented the first effort to deal with questions across denominational lines on a national scale. It represented complete recognition of the legitimacy of each group and provided the Jewish community as well as the War Department with rulings which were uniform and official. It helped the Jewish military personnel who were no longer dependent on individual decisiions and the confusion which they brought.

This daring effort went one step further as many of the responsa were printed in two widely distributed booklets. The committee answered questions for Jewish service personnel. It set a precedent by combining the efforts of the three major Jewish religious groups and publishing the results of these deliberations. This was a declaration that cooperation was possible when a modicum of good will existed. Unfortunately this effort eventually ceased. This can be attributed to the strengthening of denominational ties after World War II in North America and even more to the chief rabbinate of Israel which did its best to avoid any kind of cooperation among Jewish religious groups.[75] Nothing even vaguely akin occurred in the older or the newer Jewish communities around the world.

Jewish chaplains served in the British Imperial armies and other Allied Forces as well,[76] but never in the Russian armies. Jewish chaplains were to be found in the military forces of smaller nations as has been well documented for example the Canadian chaplains[77] and others.

All of this indicated the complete acceptance of military service, both when conscripted and voluntary. It also demonstrated a broad range of acceptance of rabbis within the military ranks.

THE PEOPLE AND HALAKHAH

The broad acceptance of mandatory military service expressed the will of the people. After centuries in which military service was not even a speck on the horizon, young Jews suddenly supported it enthusiastically. Military service was seen as the clearest sign of true equality; it was a symbol similar to the destruction of the ghetto walls by Napoleon's armies. It was perceived as a pathway to equal civil rights although not guaranteed, so even individuals as Ezekiel Landau whose statement began this paper saw military service in a positive light.

All of that may be the justification on the part of a young generation seeking a better life, but what about the rabbinic leadership which needed to consider the long term implications of service in the armies of non-Jewish rulers? They too viewed it as an essential move toward Emancipation. There was reluctant agreement shown by those who wrote responsa; they went much further in public utterances and sermons which fully supported Jewish soldiers.

SOME CONCLUSIONS

Jewish tradition provides no basis for military service in foreign armies, nor was this desired by any nation before modern times. The question, in other words was never raised. All of this changed toward the end of the eighteenth century with mass conscriptions; this development came unexpectedly and had to be faced quickly. The initial response of the Jewish leadership and much of the population was negative. Efforts were made to procure exemptions, but as the new national armies were hungry for manpower, they failed. Military service in national armies had to be accepted. It was soon undertaken with enthusiasm in western Europe, accompanied by new hopes for emancipation and complete equality. As with much else the orthodox rabbinic authorities adjusted themselves and accepted it, albeit reluctantly as also much later in the case of military service in the State of Israel.

Military life was not glorified. In modern Israel military leadership has become a possible path to political leadership. That has had some influence in Israel, but not on the rest of the Jewish community's view of military life. The number of Jews choosing it as a career path in the diaspora remains small.

Jews in the nineteenth century quickly accepted the modern nation state and recognized that it would provide civil rights, equality and economic opportunity. Military service was seen as an obligation which came with these rights. There was no precedent in the *halakhah* for such military service and the rabbinic tradition as we have seen. The Orthodox rabbinic authorities understood such service as a potential path to assimilation, voluntary in the western world and forced in Russia, yet they reluctantly concurred.

Reform rabbinic authorities accepted such service as an obligation of citizenship without discussion. It had to be integrated into Jewish life. That is the path which we have followed. Serving in foreign military units has thus become part of Jewish life in the Diaspora.

Serving military service in foreign armies has made the basic halakhic concepts of mandatory and permissive wars irrelevant. Whether a war is obligatory or discretionary has become a matter of private opinion. However, serious halakhic discussions are necessary to shape these individual views.

Now two centuries after Emancipation and military service in nation state, it would be helpful to provide a halalhic understanding for what has occurred. We need to restate our views of warfare and place them into our understanding of contemporary Judaism in the diaspora and Israel. No Jewish military theory exists in contemporary Judaism.

NOTES

1. This took place in May, 1789. Ezekiel Landau, *Meassef*, quoted in Simon Dubnow, *Die neuste Geschichte des juedischen Volkes*, Berlin, vol. 8, pp. 28-29. Emperor Joseph II's edict demanding military service (1788) imposed a heavy burden without extending civil rights. It was the first time that Jews had been inducted into a Christian army and was not welcomed by the military aristocracy either. Dubnow also noted that the Austrian army was the first to allow Jews to rise in the lower ranks.

2. Joseph Karo's *Shulhan Arukh* contians only scattered references and no entire section on this topic as he limited himself to matters which were relevant in the diaspora and did not treat anything else. This is also true of other codification. Only Maimonides *Mishneh Torah* contains a section on kings and warfare as he wished to cover all of Jewish law, even items which were theoretical or would only be possible in a future Jewish state. However, this section was far briefer than everything else discussed in his work.

3. Alfred S. Cohen, "On Yeshiva Men Serving in the Army," *Journal of Halacha and Contemporary Society*, No. 23, pp. 5 ff. presents this discussion from an Orthodox point of view.

4. Shlomoh Goren, *Meshiv Milkhamah*, Jerusalem, 1983, 2 vols. Is a good example of a practical manual; there are others of varying length. Some are intended to be carried by the soldier into combat and so very concise. In addition many discussions which apply to Israeli situations continue to appear in Hebrew periodicals. For example *Techumin*, 1983, Vol. 4 and later which devote large sections to military question. For a fuller list see Nahum Rakover, *Otzar Hamishpat*, Jerusalem, Part 1, 1970, Part 2, 1990.

5. For the beginning of th emancipation process see Walter Jacob, "Napoleon's Sanhedrin and the Halakhah," in Walter Jacob (ed.) *Napoleon's Influence on Jewish Law*, Pittsburgh, 2007, pp. 1-64.

6. The German biblical scholar von Rad tried to organize the very different accounts into a system which is interesting, but problematic. D. Gerhard von Rad, *Der Heilige Krieg im alten Israel*, Goettingen, 1958.

7. Y.K.Miklischansky, "The Israelite Army in Ancient Times," *Sefer Yovel for Israel Elfenbein*, (ed. Y. L. Maimon), Jerusalem, 1963, pp. 105-123 (Hebrew) presents a slightly longer overview.

8. I Maccabees 2:19-40 described the massacre which occurred when Jews refused to fight on shabbat and the decision to fight on shabbat. Josephus also mentioned this change. The rabbinic literature confirms the policy (Erub 45a). The Letter of Aristeas reports the enforcement of very strict shabbat observance, but deals primarily with trading and the exclusion of merchants from a walled city on shabbat.

9. I Maccabees 5:21-28; 7:47; 9:37-42; 11:47 ff. II Maccabees 5:11 ff.'12:1 ff. Josephus, *Antiquities of the Jews*, XIII, v; *War of the Jews* I, xviii and elsewhere in both books.

10. The royal family of the Chazar kingdom (740-969 C.E.) converted to Judaism under Bulan and slowly others joined them. This became known through the correspondence of the Spanish Jewish statesman, Hasdai ibn Shaprut with the last Chazar leader. Recent studies have illuminated aspects of their history, but none of this had any influence on Jewish life.

11. Louis Ginzberg, *The Legends of the Jews* (Philadelphia, 1928, VI [Notes]

12. The following matters were found in other sections. Female prisoners could be married after following the biblical prescriptions (Yeb 48b). The prisoners of war became slaves (Git 38a). Booty taken (San 20b) was divided between the ruler and the soldiers. Soldiers were permitted to eat food found in the enemy's

possession, even if it was normally ritually forbidden (Hul 17a).

13. Even a brief review of the boundaries presented in the various biblical books reveals enormous discrepancies. During my studies for the rabbinate at the Hebrew Union College I was almost tempted by a prize essays which demanded that these boundaries be investigated. A brief exploratory view of the topic revealed its complexity and I did not proceed further.

14. *Mishneh Torah, Hil. Melakhim Umilhamoteihem* 4, 5, 6.

15. For royal as well as judiciary expanded and emergency powers see *Hil. Melakhim* 3:8-10; *Hil. Mamrim* 2:4 f.

16. *Orah Hayyim, Hilkhot Shabbat* 249.

17. *Bet Yosef (Karo) and Bayit Hadash* (Sirkes)to *Orah Hayyim* 249.

18. *Letter of Aristeas* 13 stated that 30,000 Jews transported to Egypt "were armed and settled as garrisons in the country districts." He continued that earlier others had helped Psammetichus II (595 B.C.E.) against the Ethiopians.

19. *Milei D'avut Hoshen Mishpat* 4.

20. Yitzhak Baer, *A History of the Jews in Christian Spain*, Philadelphia, 1961, Vol. 1, pp. 59 f., 114, 175, 359, 368, 397.

21. Ibid., p. 389.

22. Marcus, *Op. Cit.*, p. 297.

23. Solomon bar Samson (1140) cited by Jacob R. Marcus, *Op. Cit.*, p. 115.

24. Benjamin of Tudela, quotes in Marcus, *Op. Cit.* p. 248.

25. A summary acount may be found in Max L. Margolis and Alexander Marx, *A History of the Jewish People*, Philadelphia, 1953, pp. 359 ff. For a summary of the better known sources, see the notes in H. Graetz, *Geschichte der Juden*, Leipzig, 1861, Vol. 6, pp. 424-434 and Jacob R. Marcus, *The Jew in the Medieval World - A Source Book*, Cincinnati, 1938, pp. 115-120.

26. Yitzhak se-ev Kahana, *"Shirut Hatzavah Besafrut Hateshuvot,"* *Mehakrim Besafrut Hateshuvot*, Jerusalem, 1973, pp. 164 f.

27. *Responsa Maharam*, # 43 cited by Jacob R. Marcus, *The Jew in the Medieval World*, pp. 327 ff.

28. *Or Zarua*, 593:98; *Tzemah Tzedek* 58, 59. A good summary may be found in Salo W. Baron, *A Social and Religious History of the Jews*, Philadelphia 1957, Vol. iv, pp. 197 ff; Selma Stern Tauebler, *The Court Jew*, Philadelphia, 1950, and other studies.

29. Christon I. Archer, John R. Ferris, Holger H. Herwig, H.E. Travers, *World History of Warfare*, Lincoln: University of Nebraska Press, 2002, pp. 302 ff. , 355 ff.

30. Jacob R. Marcus, *The Colonial American Jews 1492-1776*, Detroit, 1970, vol. 1, pp. 223 f. Excerpts from documents of the period may be found in Morris U Schappes (ed.), *A Documentary History of the Jews in the United States 1654-1875*, New York, 1971, pp. 1 ff.

31. Dubnow, *Op. Cit.*,vol. 8, p. 136, see also section 19.

32. Martin Philippson, *"Der Anteil der juedischen Freiwilligen an dem Berfreiungskriege* 1813 und 1814," *Monatsschrift fuer Geschichte und Wissenschaft des Judentums*, 1906, vol. 50, pp. 1 ff. See also Bernhard R. Kroener, *Weshalb kaempft ihr mit ihnen*, Berlin, 2007, p. 10.

33. Mordecai Breuer, *Modernity within Tradition - A Social History of Orthodox Jewry in Imperial Germany*, New York, 1992, p. 318.

34. Werner T. Angress, "Prussia's Army and the Jewish Reserve Officer Controversy before World War I," *Yearbook XVII of the Leo Baeck Institute*, London, New York, 1972, vol. 17, pp. 5 ff.

35. German Soldier count....Frank Naegler (ed.) *Deutsche Juedische Soldaten*, Hamburg, Berlin, E. S. Mittler, 1996.

36. *Deutsche Staatsbuerger juedischen Glaubens in der Bundeswehr*, Berlin, 2009, 32 pp. My thanks to Rabbi Walter Homolka for making me aware of this booklet.

37. Erwin A. Schmidl, *Juden in der k. (u.) k. Armee.*

38. Zosa Szajkowski, *Jews and the French Foreign Legion*, New York, 1975, xviii, 280 pp.

39. Simon Wolf, *The American Jew as Patriot, Soldier and Citizen* (ed. Louis Edward Levy), New York, 1895, 676 pp.

40. Dubnow, *Op. Cit.*, vol. 9, pp. 194-95.

41. Simon Dubnow, *History of the Jews in Russia and Poland*, Philadelphia, 1946, Vol. 2, pp. 13 ff. provides a summary of the edicts, their execution, and a vivid description of the suffering endured.

42. The length of military service changed through the decades beginning in 1805 when the obligation was first imposed. Cantonists represented a special set of problems. These were the sons of Russian Jewish soldiers, who were placed in special schools beginning in 1805, to be trained as future Russian soldiers (statute, September 1827) with an emphasis on conversion to the Greek Orthodox Church. Conditions in these schools were dreadful and aroused much sympathy in Western Europe. The system was not abolished until 1857.

43. *Noda Niyehuda Mahadura Tanina, Yoreh Deah* 74.

44. *Ibid.,* citing *Hil. Yesodei Torah* 5:5; based on *Jerushalmi Terumot* 8.4.

45. *Meir Ish, Yoreh Deah* 52.

46. Hatam Sofer, *Likutei Hatam Sofer* 29.

47. David Hoffman, *Orah Hahayim*, 42-43.

48. *Mahari Yehudah Yaaleh* 2:24

49. *Imrei Esh #* 52.

50. *Noda Biyehuda Tanina, Yoreh Deah*, 74.

51. "Introduction,"*Mahanei Yisrael.* In later chapters (38 and 39) he dealt with the role of prayer in strengthening the battle weary soldier.

52. *Tel Talpiyot Mevitzon* 1916, p. 174.

53. Eliezer Waldenberg *Responsa Even Haezer #* 6.

54. *Bet David #* 72.

55. *Shoel Umeshiv,* 1:144

56. *Teshuvot* 1:87

57. Mordecai Benet, *Parashat Mordecai*,173.

58. *Imrei Esh 2 Even Haezer* 25.

59. *Divrei Hayyim, Even Haezer*, vol. 1.4; vol. 2:64.

60. *Yehudah Yaalei* vol. 2:16.

61. *Shaarei Deah* vol. 2:182.

62. *K'tav Sofer Even Haezer* 32.

63. *Even Haezer* 51.

64. *Maharam Schick*, # 175.

65. *Mahanei Hayyim, Even Haezer,* vol. 2:17.

66. A discussion of this and other related issues has been well summarized in Yitzhak Zeev Kahana, *Mehakrim Bessafrut Hateshuvot*, pp. 175-194.

67. For Austria-Hungary see Erwin A. Schmidl, *Juden in der k. (u.) k. Armee*, pp. 198 f. For Germany see *Deutsche Juedische Soldaten*, pp. 69 f. For the United States, see Hoenig "The Orthodox Rabbi as a Military Chaplain," *Tradition*, Vol. 16, No. 2, 1976, pp. 35-60.

68. David Hoffman, *Melamed Lehoil*, New York, 1954, Vol. I, # 42, 43

69. Ismar Elbogen, *A Century of Jewish Life*, Philadelphia, 1944, pp. 454 ff.

70. Alexander Carlebach, "A German Rabbi goes East," *Year Book VI of the Leo Baeck Institute*, New York, 1961, pp. 110 ff. This essay consists of a selection of letters from Rabbi Carlebach to his family during his stay in Warsaw from 1916 to 1918. He provides a vivid description of the condition of Polish Jewry and the many efforts of the German occupation forces to be helpful.

71. Mordecai Breuer, *Modernity within Tradition*, pp. 388 f.

72. Bertram Korn, American Jewry and the Civil War, Philadelphia, 1951, p. 68; Jack D. Foner, "Jews and the American Military from the Colonial Era to the Eve of the Civil War," *American Jewish Archives Journal*, Vol. 52, No. 1-2, pp. 54-111.

73. Ibid., pp. 56-97. See also Harry Simonoff, *Jewish Participants in the Civil War*, New York, 1963, pp. 36 ff "The Orthodox Rabbi as a Military Chaplain," *Tradition*, Vol. 16, No. 2, 1976, pp. 35-60.

74. Sidney B. Hoenig, "The Orthodox Rabbi as a Military Chaplain," *Tradition*, Vol. 16, No. 2, 1976, pp. 35-60 provides a good summary of the early history as well as an Orthodox perspective.

75. In the 1970s I was involved along with a representative of the American Conservative and Orthodox movements in an effort to agree on conversion procedures with the Israeli chief rabbinate. We met for a week in Jerusalem with a representative of the chief rabbinate, worked on an agreement, hammered out its wording, began to translate it from Hebrew into English, when at the last minute the chief rabbinate backed out. Aside from a pleasant visit to Israel and the rare books of the Schocken Library where the meetings were held, nothing was accomplished except a distrust of any future cooperative efforts with the Israeli rabbinate.

76. *Responsa in Wartime*, (ed. National Jewish Welfare Board), New York, 1947, 96 pp.

77. S. Gershon Levi, *Breaking New Ground: The Struggle for a Jewish Chaplaincy in Canada*, ed. David Golinkin, Montreal, 1994.

FIGHTING IN THE ISRAELI ARMY

Walter Jacob

War marked the birth of Israel and fighting has been continuous through the decades. After two thousand years of self-imposed pacifism a vigorous militancy was born. It was necessity, not a fighting ideology which brought this about. Israel became an independent state on May 14, 1948 and established its military forces on the same day. David Ben-Gurion, the Defense minister formed this conscript army out of the paramilitary Hagganah, Palmach, and units of Irgun and Lehi. He had quietly developed a structure through 1947 as he knew that Arab attacks would come immediately, as they did. These defense forces actually began in 1907 as Bar Giora which, along with its successor organizations was intended to provide protection for the settlements against marauders. During World War I a Jewish Legion and a Zion Mule Corps assisted the British. A defense force was created in April 1920 during the first Arab riots; it was expanded in the 1936–1939 riots and eventually formed the basis of the Hagganah. The Israeli armed forces have fought a major war along with numerous small engagements in every decade since the creation of the State.

How was this new military entity to fit into the Jewish thought and the halakhah. No Jewish armed forces had existed for thousands of years and Jews fighting for other lands also represented a new experience as demonstrated in an earlier essay in this volume. The traditional halakhah provided virtually no guidance for the troops or the leadership of newly independent Israel.

If placed into a halalkhic setting, the entire struggle could be seen as *milhemet mitzvah* (mandatory commanded war), a struggle to defend the new state and its people – the land as provided by United Nations Resolution and expanded through the defeat of aggressive, attacking neighbors. When viewed through the lens of ancient biblical Israel the pattern, unfortunately has been very much the same. Although many of the modern settlers came from the sea, not from the desert, possession of the land was similarly contested and a cessation of hostilities never endured long.

The Messianic dream of a divinely established peaceful resolution to the struggles brought hope to war-torn biblical Israel. In the subsequent centuries when Jews lived in other lands or without freedom in the land of the Bible, it brought a vision of a wonderful future. This dream was sufficed during centuries of political powerlessness both within and outside the Land of Israel. Prophets and mystics hoped that God would fulfill the dream. Perhaps it would occur through a miraculous, sudden heavenly intervention in the affairs of the world. Others thought that a divine cataclysmic end of the world would destroy all evil and bring peace. A few understood themselves as Messianic ambassadors through whom the vision of a world perfectly at peace would be realized. All witnessed the horrors of warfare with helpless dismay. Each despaired of any human solution.

Contemporary Jews, however, refuse to despair; modern Jews, both religious and secular are less passive and want to take part in efforts toward peace and not simply wait. The creation of Israel along with two centuries of Jewish partnership in social revolutions in the diaspora testify to this optimistic impatience. Some have seen themselves as partners with God. This approach is less utopian and begins where we are; in the case of warfare, not the elimination of war, but mitigating its effects. Along with many others this has led to forming rules of warfare which attempt to control soldiers even in the midst of the fighting. Treaties among nations have limited the destructive effects of war and occupation on the general population. The mass slaughter of innocent bystanders around the world in the previous century have moved us in this direction. We know that civilian casualties in the wars of the twentieth and twenty-first centuries have vastly outnumbered military dead.

The Israeli armed forces had to begin anew, set standards, and provide guidelines. When viewed broadly, we see that they reflect the ethical basis of the halakhah. We can and should endorse the path set by Israel for its armed force. That path is simple and direct. As the millennia of traditional material was sparse, starting anew was appropriate.

The Israelis were creative just as traditional Judaism has always been inventive, as we have learned from modern historical studies. Eventually those innovations were incorporated into the tradition and the talmudic scholars even discovered Scriptural bases for most of them. Modern Judaism has been equally inventive as the efforts of Reform and Conservative Judaism have demonstrated. These movements created new responses to unfulfilled needs of modern Jews. That is precisely what the Israeli armed forces have done.

Israel did not create entirely *de novo*, but followed other nations as it developed a code of conduct for its military forces. This code assures a level of humanity in the face of modern, impersonal combat It forms the basis upon which a broader Jewish approach to warfare can be shaped. It does not ask some of the basic questions and leaves them to the philosophers while engaging the practical conduct of warfare.

This code of military conduct, similar to those of other nations is secular, but depends upon fundamental human feelings, often religious, to carry them into practice. That has been done successfully with the United States military code, which is also secular, but depends on military chaplains of all denominations to instil its ideas into the soldier's daily conduct. The code of military conduct of the State of Israel is a moral document and should take its place in Jewish ethical and halakhic discussions.

BACKGROUND

The Israeli military forces are the first Jewish military units under the command of a Jewish state in two thousand years. This military force differs in many ways from its distant predecessor. It is a conscript force with a small professional core, made up of men, who serve three years and women who serve twenty-one months with reserve training every year till the age of fifty-one. Emergency call-ups may and do occur at any time. The military services ultimately serve under the direction of the ministry created by the Parliament (*Kenesset*). The designation, Israeli Defense Forces (*Tzahal*) indicates its mission and limits.

Through the decades, these military forces have played a significant role in creating a cohesive nation. Israel formed itself rapidly through blending its native born citizens with large numbers of immigrants from a wide range of countries and cultures. As each group's natural inclination was to remain separate, only the mandatory military service brought everyone together. This remains an important task in shaping a national identity.

Theoretically all young people serve in the military, however, men of the *haredi* (ultra Orthodox) community may defer military service while studying in a *yeshivah*; this has generally meant indefinitely and continues to be a source of great friction and animosity. This system of deferral was originally granted by Ben Gurion for what he understood to be a limited, small group, approximately four hundred men. The deferral now excludes tens of thousands, approximately 50,000, growing from about 7% of the eighteen-year-old cohort ten years ago, to some 14% today, and an anticipated 25% in twelve years. Women who claim a "religious life style" are also exempt from service. Efforts continue to be made to induce participation in military service through a special infantry unit, but with little effect. Similarly, efforts to recruit *haredi* men to alternative "National Service" have had meager results.

The *hesder* system has been more successful; it consists of a five year program with one year of religious studies, followed by two years of military service and two years of religious studies with the responsibility for active duty whenever emergencies demand it. This has, however, created a new challenge as shown by the recent debates whether rabbinic edicts supplant military commands, an intolerable situation for any army.[1]

Obligatory War *Milhemet Mitzvah*

As the basic nature of the Israeli military forces is defensive, it fits into the classic definition of "mandatory war" (*mikhemet mitzvah*) performed at the command of the ruler; in our time a prime minister elected and beholden to the *knesset*. While the halakhic authorities debate this conclusion, most Israelis would agree with this classification although they may have little or no interest in a *halakhic* defintion.

Milhemet reshut, a "permissive war" according to talmudic tradition required the assent of a court of twenty-three along with consultation of the *Urim* and *Tumim* has no modern parallel though the *knesset* could be considered as a substitute for a court of twenty-three. Maimonides following the Talmud, understood the limits of these abstract discussions.[2] The power of the ruler to defend the nation or to meet emergencies was unquestioned. All governments must possess room for discretion in their conduct especially of military and foreign affairs. *Milhemet reshut* provides that when redefined, if it is to serve a modern useful purpose.

It is in the category of *milhemet reshut* that has brought problems to the Israeli Defense Forces. Soldiers who served without protest in the defense of Israel, were unwilling to engage, in what they considered an offensive war, as with Lebanon in 2003. This continues to be debated in the *hesder yeshivot*, which may have unacceptable results. The Israeli soldier, like all citizens, of course has the opportunity to express his views through the ballot, but not on the field of combat.

MILITARY LAW AND CONDUCT

Israeli military law has largely followed international codes of conduct which have been incorporated into its system. These have been integrated along with specific Israeli legislation and Jewish traditions as interpreted by the Israeli courts and the military tribunals.

Jewish tradition provides virtually no details except the conscription statements of Deuteronomy along with the few others. These became the object of academic discourses unrelated to real life situations.[3] This meant that every aspect of the soldier's governance had to be created anew. Some standards for religious ritual and relationships with fellow soldiers have been developed by Israeli military chaplains under the guidance of Rabbi Goren, the chief chaplain. These provide guidance, not governance for the individual's personal life. Clear and direct statements which deal with conduct during hostilities, the treatment of enemy personnel, dealing with civilians in hostile territories, etc. were needed and provided by the general code of conduct.

The code which was developed defines three core values for all IDF soldiers, as well as ten secondary values (the first is most important, and the others are sorted in Hebrew alphabetical order):

CORE VALUES

Defense of the State, its Citizens and its Residents – "The IDF's goal is to defend the existence of the State of Israel, its independence and the security of the citizens and residents of the state."

Love of the Homeland and Loyalty to the Country – "At the core of service in the IDF stand the love of the homeland and the commitment and devotion to the State of Israel–a democratic state that serves as a national home for the Jewish People – its citizens and residents."

Human Dignity – "The IDF and its soldiers are obligated to protect human dignity. Every human being is of value regardless of his or her origin, religion, nationality, gender, status or position."

OTHER VALUES

Tenacity of Purpose in Performing Missions and Drive to Victory "The IDF servicemen and women will fight and conduct themselves with courage in the face of all dangers and obstacles; They will persevere in their missions resolutely and thoughtfully even to the point of endangering their lives."

Responsibility – "The IDF servicemen or women will see themselves as active participants in the defense of the state, its citizens and residents. They will carry out their duties at all times with initiative, involvement and diligence with common sense and within the framework of their authority, while prepared to bear responsibility for their conduct."

Credibility – "The IDF servicemen and women shall present things objectively, completely and precisely, in planning, performing and reporting. They will act in such a manner that their peers and commanders can rely upon them in performing their tasks."

Personal Example – "The IDF servicemen and women will comport themselves as required of them, and will demand of themselves as they demand of others, out of recognition of their ability and responsibility within the military and without to serve as a deserving role model."

Human Life – "The IDF servicemen and women will act in a judicious and safe manner in all they do, out of recognition of the supreme value of human life. During combat they will endanger themselves and their comrades only to the extent required to carry out their mission."

Purity of Arms – "The soldier shall make use of his weaponry and power only for the fulfillment of the mission and solely to the extent required; he will maintain his humanity even in combat. The soldier shall not employ his weaponry and power in order to harm non-combatants or prisoners of war, and shall do all he can to avoid harming their lives, body, honor and property."

Professionalism – "The IDF servicemen and women will acquire the professional knowledge and skills required to perform their tasks, and will implement them while striving continuously to perfect their personal and collective achievements."

Discipline – "The IDF servicemen and women will strive to the best of their ability to fully and successfully complete all that is required of them according to orders and their spirit. IDF soldiers will be meticulous in giving only lawful orders, and shall refrain from obeying blatantly illegal orders."

Comradeship – "The IDF servicemen and women will act out of fraternity and devotion to their comrades, and will always go to their assistance when they need their help or depend on them, despite any danger or difficulty, even to the point of risking their lives."

Sense of Mission – "The IDF soldiers view their service in the IDF as a mission; They will be ready to give their all in order to defend the state, its citizens and residents. This is due to the fact that they are representatives of the IDF who act on the basis and in the framework of the authority given to them in accordance with IDF orders." [4]

As the military forces primarily deal with Palestinians, a special section of the code treat this matter.

CODE OF CONDUCT AGAINST MILITANTS AND PALESTINIAN CIVILIANS

In 2004 a team of professors, commanders and former judges, led by the holder of the Ethics chair at Tel Aviv University, Professor Asa Kasher, developed a code of conduct which emphasizes the right behavior in low intensity warfare against terrorists, where soldiers must operate within a civilian population. Reserve units and regular units alike are taught the following eleven rules of conduct, which are an addition to the more general *IDF Spirit*:

1. Military action can be taken only against military targets.

2. The use of force must be proportional.

3. Soldiers may only use weaponry they were issued by the IDF.

4. Anyone who surrenders cannot be attacked.

5. Only those who are properly trained can interrogate prisoners.

6. Soldiers must accord dignity and respect to the Palestinian population and those arrested.

7. Soldiers must give appropriate medical care, when conditions allow, to oneself and one's enemy.

8. Pillaging is absolutely and totally illegal.

9. Soldiers must show proper respect for religious and cultural sites and artifacts.

10. Soldiers must protect international aid workers, including their property and vehicles.

11. Soldiers must report all violations of this code.[5]

These codes of military conduct and their specific definitions generally follow those of other lands, adjusted for Israeli conditions. They provide the basis for conduct for twenty-first century warfare. They reflect broad international consensus. Rabbinic sources have been specifically excluded to avoid the internal religious conflicts of modern Israel.

This code provides a basis for proper conduct in practical field situations. It is intended for all Israeli soldiers no matter what their religious inclinations. Some will view it through the lens of the halakhah. Others may want to go further in the spirit of the ancient prophets. Still others will see it as a secular document of their society. It represents a voice of modern variegated Judaism

This code moves in the appropriate direction and fills a vacuum in the traditional halakhah. The standards set by the IDF are based on general assumptions and fit into the Jewish frame-work. They are practical, enforceable and represent standards which parallel those of many other nations. The major distinction is the that they continue to be tested on the battlefield as the Israeli Defense Forces have been more or less in continuous combat for seven decades. The standards may not reach the highest ideals, but they are adequate and as all standards need vigilant enforcement. We may well feel that they need modification and that will undoubtedly occur as new conditions are faced and as experience teaches, but they represent a good faith beginning.

The Israeli legislation and policies of the occupation and the numerous issues surrounding the West Bank lie beyond the scope of this paper.

The IDF represents a practical expression of Israeli defense policy. We would not expect it to provide a broader, general philosophy of war and peace. Such considerations involve the ultimate aims of all wars, the limits of defense, the conditions of pre-emptive war, and related matters. Each of these and related matters are basic to an understanding of war in an Israeli Jewish context.

The state of continual warfare and the need for defense as well as constant vigilance has muted discussions of the broader issues of war and peace They remain difficult to carry out in Israel, a land which has not known enough peace to be able to step away from the practical, immediate considerations. The ideal of peace remains, but so does warfare. Israel along with other nations which are part of the United Nations must continually seek ways of settling disputes outside the realm of active warfare.

Notes

1. Among other sources, some of those on the internet are most useful. My thanks to my friend and colleague, Uri Regev for leading me to these sources. http://www.jpost.com/servlet/Satellite?cid=1261364566025&pagename=JPost/J PArticle/ShowFull; RLINK"http://www.ynetnews.com/articles/0,7340,L-3819361,00.html" http://www.ynetnews.com/articles/0,7340,L-3819361,00.html

2. Maimonides, in accordance with the Talmud gave extra-legal judicial authority to the courts (Yev 90b; *Mishneh Torah*, Mamrim 2:4)) in unusual cases and to the ruler (San 49a 57a; *Mishneh Torah*, San 57a; Melakhim 3:8 and 10; 9:14). http://www.yutorah.org/_shiurim/Succot-To-Go%205767.pdf – towards the end of the document. http://www.jlaw.com/Articles/war1.html

3. See the Introduction to this volume for a summary.

4.   Wikepidia "Ethics - the IDF Spirit.   IDF Spokesperson's Unit (http://dover.odf.il/IDF/English/about/doctrine/ethics.htm" Along with other public sources have been used for the English translations.

5. Wikepidia, p. 13. No attempt has been made to list the numerous books, essays, and articles which have dealt with the legal discussions surrounding the occupation nor the restrictions placed upon the Palestinians.

SELECTED RESPONSA

The responsa on the following pages represent a selection taken from a century of American Reform responsa along with special war-time reponsa. We are grateful to the Central Conference of American Rabbis Press and the Hebrew Union College Press for permission to republish these responsa. They have been presented as previously published with no effort to change the Hebrew transliteration or their style.

REDEMPTION OF CAPTIVES
2003

QUESTION: What does Jewish tradition teach us concerning the ransom of captives? Specifically, both Maimonides (*Yad,* Hilkhot Matanot Aniyim 8:10) and the *Shulchan Arukh* (Yore Deah 252:3) indicate that we must pay the ransom and negotiate with those who take hostages. What can we learn from these teachings that might help us shape an appropriate response to those who would kidnap Jews for any purpose? (Rabbi Douglas E. Krantz, Armonk, NY).

ANSWER: Jewish tradition indeed speaks directly to this issue which is, regrettably, of more than theoretical interest to the Jewish community, whether in Israel or elsewhere.

The Talmud refers to the redemption of captives (*pidyon shevuyim*) as a high obligation, greater even than that of *tzedakah*.[1] Maimonides, in the passage cited above, expresses the Talmudic law as follows: "The redemption of captives takes precedence over supporting the poor...One who ignores the responsibility to redeem the captive violates the following negative commandments: 'Do not harden your heart and do not shut your hand [from your brother in need]' (Deut. 15:7); 'do not stand idly by the blood of your neighbor'(Lev. 19:16); 'he (the master) shall not rule rigorously over him [the indentured servant]' (Lev. 25:33). He similarly annuls a number of positive commandments: 'You shall surely open your hand to him' (Deut. 15:8); 'your brother shall live with you' (Lev. 25:36); 'you shall love your neighbor as yourself' (Lev. 19:18)... There is no *mitzvah* as great as the redemption of captives." The *Shulhan Arukh* notes: "Each instant that one fails to redeem captives when it is possible to do so, it is as though one has shed blood."[2]

Yet despite its exalted status, this obligation is not without limits. The Mishnah[3] instructs that we are not to redeem captives "for more than their monetary value" (*yoter al kedey demeyhen*)[4] on account of "the welfare of society" (*mipney tikun ha-olam*). What could "welfare" mean in this context? The Talmud[5] offers two explanations: Payment of exorbitant ransoms might bankrupt the community; alternately, the knowledge that the Jews will pay dearly to redeem their captives might tempt would-be kidnappers to seize more Jewish hostages.

There is a significant halakhic difference between these two explanations. Should we conclude that ransoms are limited due to the crushing burden they impose upon community treasuries, then there would be no restriction imposed upon the amount that wealthy individuals may pay out of their own funds to redeem their relatives. On the other hand, should we adopt the second theory, concern that high ransom payments encourage further kidnappings, then even the wealthy would be prohibited from paying more than the limit set by the Mishnah.[6]

The Talmud does not resolve this issue, and the halakhic authorities are in dispute. The Rambam declares that ransoms are limited in order to discourage future kidnappings.[7] R. Asher ben Yechiel,[8] by contrast, rules that a private individual may exceed the ransom limit in order to redeem himself, his wife,[9] or a Torah scholar.[10] Others expand the permit, allowing an individual to redeem any family member at any price.[11] Such lenient rulings would imply that the limitation was instituted to safeguard the public treasury. The *Shulhan Arukh* strikes a balance between these alternatives: it simultaneously accepts Rambam's explanation for the ransom limitation *and* R. Asher's exceptions to the rule.[12]

While some, if not all, of these authorities permit individuals to exceed the Mishnah's limitation upon ransom payments, none of them allows the community to do so. This distinction between the private and the public realms is eminently reasonable. The primary ethical responsibility of individuals, when confronting the captivity of loved ones, is to the captives themselves; that duty may be said to take precedence over their responsibilities toward society at large.[13] Governments, meanwhile, may not set such priorities; they are charged with the protection of the entire community. As such, they are forbidden to yield to the extortionate sums demanded by the kidnappers, for to do so would encourage future attempts at hostage-taking and thereby expose the rest of their citizens to danger.

The government of Israel, in its dealings with hostage-takers, wrestles with the very dynamic described in the rabbinic sources. Though the question may not involve the "monetary value" of captives, it does go to the issue of price: at what point do the demands of the kidnappers become "unreasonable," so that the government, which is ultimately responsible for the security of the people as a whole, must refuse to give in to them? In return for prisoners of war or civilian hostages, captors will set an exorbitant price, often the release of hundreds of imprisoned terrorists or criminals for each liberated Israeli. To yield to this demand might well entice other potential kidnappers to seize captives in the future; the freed prisoners, in addition, would pose a serious security risk to the Israeli public. The government may regard this price as excessive and, faced with a choice between the lives and freedom of its captive citizens and the safety of its population as a whole, refuse to pay it. Difficult as this decision must be, it is well in keeping with the Jewish legal tradition which, in the name of *tikun ha-olam*, sets limits on what communities may pay to redeem their captives.

Still, a case can be made for the opposing view, that no demand is too excessive or unreasonable when the lives of the captives are at stake. Some authorities rule that the limits imposed upon ransom payments apply only when the captors are interested solely in money. When they threaten to kill their hostages, however, the commandment to save life (*pikuah nefesh*) takes precedence over all else. While others disagree,[14] this theory has been adopted by a leading contemporary halakhist, R. Ovadiah Yosef,[15] who argues that in such instances the clear and present danger (*vadai sakanah*) to the lives of the hostages outweighs the potential danger (*safek sakanah*) to the rest of the population should the ransom be paid. On this basis Yosef concludes that Israel ought to pay the price, whatever it may be, which terrorists demand for the release of its captive citizens.

His opinion, however, is subject to a number of criticisms. First, it is by no means clear under Jewish law that individuals or societies are required (or even permitted) to subject themselves to *safek sakanah* in order to rescue those in *vadai sakanah*.[16]

Second, it is arguable that the danger posed to society by the payment of exorbitant ransoms, while not as direct as that to the hostages, is no less "certain."[17]

Third, R. Yosef bases his argument in part upon his claim that by giving in to terrorist demands we do not thereby invite further intimidation, since the terrorists are committed to a campaign of violence and murder against Israel and its people whether we give in to their demands or not. He may be right; still, much political and strategic thinking disputes him, holding that surrender to the demands of hostage-takers *does* encourage future acts of violence.

Fourth, R. Yosef does not consider the fact that Israel is a sovereign nation in a state of war with its neighbors. Since its enemies have shown themselves willing to pursue this war against its civilian population, it is not unreasonable for Israel to regard all its citizens as soldiers in the conflict. If soldiers are called upon to risk their lives in defense of the nation, Israel's civilian hostages may be said to share that duty. R. Yosef's ruling is, to be sure, a compassionate one; he would place the safe return of hostages in the first rank of Israeli security priorities. In so doing, however, he would tie the hands of Israel's civilian and military leaders who must somehow, in painful dilemmas such as these, strike an acceptable balance between the lives of the hostages and the welfare of an entire nation.

This balance, we think, can be established solely on a case-by-case basis. In any hostage situation, the government must determine whether and to what extent payment of the ransom demanded by the kidnappers would threaten the safety of the rest of the population. In some situations the government will decide that to pay the ransom is the lesser of two evils, that to obtain the freedom of its captives justifies whatever danger the public may face at some later date.[18] In others, it will conclude that the price is too high. In each case, the decision must reflect, on the strength of careful consultation with military, diplomatic, and political experts, the best available judgement as to the likely results of either course of action.[19]

This is no guarantee that mistakes will not be made; experts, like the rest of us, can be wrong. It is, however, the surest means by which the government of Israel (and indeed, any government or communal authority) can hope to discharge its ethical responsibilities to its people against the backdrop of one of the harshest realities of our time.

Notes

1. Baba Batra 8a-b.

2. Yore De'ah 252:3. The source is *Responsa* R. Yosef Kolon (Maharik, 15th-century Italy), # 7.

3. Gitin 4:6.

4. How to determine the "monetary value" of captives is a subject of some dispute. Some (Chidushey ha-Ritba, Gittin 45a) set the amount according to the price the individual would fetch on the slave market (or the estimated price, should slavery no longer be in practice; *Responsa* Maharam Lublin, # 15). Others (*Responsa* R. David ibn Zimra *Ha-Chadashot*, # 40) measure the ransom price against that which is normally paid to kidnappers. Still others (*Responsa* Menachem Ha-Meiri, *Beit Ha-Bechirah*, Ketubot 52b) set the price according to the captive's social status.

5. Gittin 45a.

6. Rashi, Gittin 45a, s.v. *o'dilma*.

7. *Yad*, Hilkhot Matanot Aniyim 8:12. Alfasi, Ketubot 52b (fol. 19a), rules that a husband may not redeem his captive wife "for more than her monetary value." This suggests that Alfasi, too, accepts the reasoning that the limits are set in order to discourage future kidnappings and that even a private individual may not exceed those restrictions; see Rabbeinu Nissim ad loc., as well as Chiddushey Ha-Rashba, Gittin 45a. This position is adopted as well by the Gaon of Vilna (*Bi'ur Ha-Gra*, Yoreh Dea 252, # 6).

8. Gittin 4:44, following Tosafot, Gittin 45a, s.v. *dela*. See also R. Asher to M.

9. Ketubot 5:22, in the name of R. Meir Halevy Abulafia. See Ketubot 52a-b.

10. See Gittin 58a, where R. Yehoshua pays a high price to redeem a child from captivity, because he realizes that the child is learned and will one day become a great halakhic sage. "How much the more so," says R. Asher, "does this apply to one who is already a talmid chakham."

11. See R. Yoel Sirkes, *Bayit Chadash* to *Tur*, Yoreh Deah 252, who notes that such is common practice "to which no one objects", and R. Shabtai Cohen, *Siftey Kohen*, Yoreh Deah 252, # 4.

12. Yoreh Deah 252:4. In Even Haezer 78:2, we read: "the husband is not obligated to redeem his wife at a price greater than her monetary value...." This suggests that he may do so if he wishes.

13. A similar order of priorities is established with regard to the giving of *tzedakah*. See Baba Metzi'a 71a (on Ex. 22:24); *Yad*, Hilkhot Matanot Aniyim 7:13; *Shulhan Arukh* Yoreh Deah 251:3.

14. See the responsa cited in *Pitchey Teshuvah*, Yoreh Deah 252, # 4.

15. In *Torah She-be'al Peh* 19 (1977), 9–39.

16. See, in general, *Journal of Reform Judaism* 36 (Winter, 1989), 53-65, and the sources cited there. R. Yosef may have the better argument on this point, yet given the long-standing dispute over the issue, it is a shaky halakhic foundation upon which to advocate that Israel cave in to extortionate ransom demands.

17. R. Ezekiel Katzenellenbogen, Resp. Kenesset Yechezkel, # 38.

18. And, contrary to popular impression, Israel has never adhered to a "no negotiations--ever" policy with respect to hostages. Its recent willingness to deal for the release of Western captives in Beirut and (thus far unsuccessfully) for its pilot Ron Arad, held by the Hezbollah in Lebanon, are cases in point.

19.This is essentially the position taken by a number of contemporary authorities. See R. Shaul Yisraeli in *Torah She-be'al Peh* 17 (1975), pp. 69-76, R. Yehudah Gershuni in *Ha-Darom* (1971), pp. 27-37, and our colleague R. Moshe Zemer in *Ha'Aretz*, December 13, 1983.

Mark Washovsky
(not previously published)

RANSOMING A KIDNAPED EXECUTIVE
1993

QUESTION: A young Jewish man has been kidnaped and has been held for ransom in a South American country. The family and the corporation for which he works are seeking his release. The American government has discouraged payment of the large ransom as it would encourage further kidnapings. The family is concerned about his health as he was abducted several months ago. What path should the family take? Is there some traditional Jewish guidance?

ANSWER: Unfortunately this is not a modern problem, but has been faced endlessly through the centuries. One of the earliest tales connected with Abraham (Gen.14) had him gathering a posse in order to force the release of his nephew Lot. He was successful. That may be an option for a government, but is clearly not the path in this instance. We should note that it was the road taken by the Israeli government in the daring and highly successful rescue at Entebe, Uganda in 1976, taken despite the disastrous effort by the German government at the Munich Olympics in 1972. Less dramatic rescue operations have also been mounted by Israeli military and by other nations in their native lands and in every area of the world.

Captives and their rescue has been a major concern of the Jewish tradition. It is considered so important that it over-rides any other concerns and is an obligation placed upon the entire community. The biblical statement of Exodus (21:16) considers kidnaping a capitol offense and imposes the death penalty. The Mishnah understood this as a common danger and so in its discussion of obligations assumed by a husband on his marriage included ransoming his wife from possible captivity (Ket. 4:8), a sad commentary on insecurity of that period. This discussion was expanded in considerable detail in the Talmud (Ket 46b, 52 a and b). Other acts of ransoming were not discussed at all, but, obviously taken for granted. The main caveat in these discussions was the caution of paying an excessive ransom expressed by R. Gamliel, so that further acts of kidnaping would not be encouraged. The obligation expressed here rested upon the family or the individual himself, if he possessed the means.

We can sense how common such acts were in the ninth and tenth centuries through the documents of the Cairo Genizah. They frequently mention, rather casually the captivity of merchants who were then rescued by their companions who were fortunate enough to escape. The issues discussed concerned the reimbursement of the sums expended by the rescuers. The obligation to come to the rescue was assumed. Furthermore when news of a Jewish captive was reported, the community assumed the obligation of rescuing him and possibly his family. This was understood as a natural obligation which was to be carried out as quickly as possible once the news became known.

The Codes of Jewish law emphasize the importance of this *mitzvah* as an obligation which over-rides virtually everything else. It has always been considered the most necessary act of *tzedakah* (charity), so both Maimonides (1135–1204) and the later Joseph Karo (1488–1575) provide a long list of biblical citations (Lev. 19:16; 18; 25:33; 36; Deut 15:7 and 8) to demonstrate its importance; the citations are more extensive than for any other *mitzvah*. For both of them this had become a communal obligation. Any and all funds available for charitable purposes were to be used for this purpose and had a primary call upon these moneys. This included funds set aside from the construction of a synagogue; it timbers and other building material had already been purchased, they were to be sold in order to free captives. If it was necessary to collect additional funds, then this was authorized. The caveat expressed by these authorities and others later, was that it be done in a way not to encourage future acts of kidnaping (*Mishneh Torah* , Matnat Aniyim 8:10 ff; *Shulhan Arukh Yoreh Deah* 252). Karo devoted an entire section to this problem.

As many issues arose about the details of carrying out this obligation, the matter continued to be discussed frequently. It occurs in the responsa literature of virtually every century. The discussions treated everything including the involvement of intermediaries, what sums were considered exorbitant, repayment of ransom moneys, the obligation of individual communities, etc. Some of these discussions reflect concerns raised after the rescue had occurred and which could then be settled at leisure. When Meir of Rothenburg (1215–1293)was held for ransom in the 13th century, his captors demanded a very high ransom as they knew that he was greatly esteemed by the Jewish communities, he refused to be ransomed and did not permit the communities to raise the sum. He was held until his death; then the wealthy admirer, Alexander Wimpfen, ransomed his body, for proper burial (Heinrich Graetz, *Geschichte der Juden* Vol. VII, pp. 173 f.; 423 f.).

All this material suggests that kidnaping for ransom was common and that Jews, as an oppressed minority, were often the target. As many were merchants and traveled, they faced greater danger than the general population. Kidnaping could frequently be undertaken without enraging the local ruler who often stood by and expressed no concern. The literature only rarely indicates any interest on the part of the government in the plight of such Jews. At times it participated in the kidnaping as with Meir of Rothenburg. The Jewish communities were left to their own devices. Rescue in a timely fashion was an absolute obligation placed upon the family and the Jewish community.

The importance of a timely rescue remains for us in our age. Fortunately the incidence of such kidnaping has become rare as the modern world is more secure. When it does occur it is a tragedy especially for the family.

The situation of our question is different as the government is friendly and seeks to protect all its citizens. In this case it has discouraged the family from acting alone. We should note that the kidnapers seem to be part of a revolutionary group which the United States government opposes which adds a political dimension. This, however, is different from an act of kidnaping by Fatah or some other group involved in the Israeli vs. Palestinian struggle. There the emphasis is on ideology and the ransom has usually be expressed in political terms (release of prisoners, etc.) and not as a matter of money.

The family in our case is concerned with the safety of their young man; it has moved slowly out of respect for the position of the government which it understands. The young man has not been visited by any government representative or by any neutral party such as the Red Cross. The photographs of him in captivity show him as alive though clearly suffering. The family was told that our government and that of the country involved would pursue this diligently and that the family as well as the corporation should not interfere as this would endanger any discussions with the captors.

The family has accepted this and followed that path so that there has been little contact with the captors. As several months have elapsed and despite constant contact with the American authorities, there is little sign of any resolution, the desperation of the family members can be understood.

As rescue of captives is such an important obligation and mandatory, the family must seek all possible paths which can further this aim. Initially it seemed best to follow the warnings of the governments and to allow them to pursue this matter quietly with the hope of success. During these months the family has avoided any publicity and has left it in the hands of the government. Since so much time has elapsed, it is appropriate to now follow the road of negotiating themselves. If they need additional help they should involve their community and the media as well. Negotiation and public pressure may assure a positive outcome.

The matter may have become so political that the local government is unwilling to move further and simply delays. Placing all of this into a much broader context may be their national interest, but we are concerned with a single individual who is not involved in the political struggle at all and is an innocent bystander

We would make a distinction between the role of the government and its broad concerns and that of the family which needs to look after the safety of a single individual. Should this person who is not involved in the revolutionary struggle and whose company is in a business which also had no impact on the revolution, suffer as an innocent cog in the wheel? Our answer would be negative, the family should proceed with all means at its disposal and rescue the individual. It should seek to do so quietly, if that is possible and so act within the boundaries set by the United States government. which have not been advisory, not mandatory.

Walter Jacob
(not previously published)

CONCEALING JEWISH IDENTITY

1985

QUESTION: Is it permissible to deny our identity as Jews if we find ourselves in a life threatening situation caused by terrorists? This question has been prompted by the events surrounding the highjacking of the *Achille Lauro* by terrorists. What should we do if we find ourselves in such a situation? Should we instruct our children to conceal their Jewish identity under such circumstances? (Rabbi S. Priesand, Tinton Falls, NJ)

ANSWER: It is a clear statement of Jewish tradition that one must give up one's life rather than violate three prohibitions. They are idolatry, incest and killing another person (San. 60 ff; A.Z. 43b, 54a; Ket. 33b; Shab. 149a; *Sefer Hazmitvot* Lo Ta-aseh #2 ff, 10 and 14; *Shulhan Arukh* Yoreh Deah 157.1). Unfortunately, this question has arisen many times, and there is considerable literature on the subject. Frequently in the Middle Ages Jews were threatened with death unless they accepted Christianity or Islam. (A good summary of the literature is provided by H.J. Zimmel's *Die Marranen in der Rabbinischen Literatur*). Many from the time of the Crusaders onward became martyrs under those circumstances.

Many from the time of the Crusaders onward became martyrs under those circumstances. Other simulated an acceptance of Christianity or Islam while they privately remained Jews and escaped when that possibility arose (W. Jacob, "Status of Children," *American Reform Responsa,* #145). Such individuals who publicly proclaimed another religion, but privately remained Jews, were to be considered Jews in most ways even though *lehat-hilah*, another course of action was mandated (*Shulhan Arukh* Yoreh Deah 119.12; Orah Hayim 128.37; Even Haezer 42.5). These were the decisions of the *Shulhan Arukh*. Earlier opinions varied according to: (a) the danger presented by such apostasy to the Jewish community; (b) the conditions under which they returned to Judaism, as I have discussed in the responsum cited above.

Maimonides (1135–1204)prohibited a feigned acceptance of another religion in accordance with the *Talmud*; no Jew was to abandon his religion for another religion (*Sefer Hamitzvot*, Ta-aseh 9), as did Caro (1488–1575) (*Shulhan Arukh* Yoreh Deah 157.1). The *Shulhan Arukh* had also stipulated very clearly that even at the risk of death, one can not declare, "I am not a Jew" (Yoreh Deah 157.2). The question of permitting apostasy was faced by Ephraim Oshry (*Responsa Mema-amakim* 13) and others during the Holocaust. And he answered it negatively, and stated that a Jew may not save himself through the purchase of a forged baptismal certificate, and thereby, try to join the partisans in the forest. However, there is also another line of thought which states that if a Jew is able to provide an ambiguous answer, which does not require an outright declaration that he is a Christian, such a declaration is considered acceptable (Isserles to *Shulhan Arukh* Yoreh Deah 157.2, in accord with *Nimukei Yosef*).

There were also instances, particularly in the medieval period, in which Jews wore Christian garb to save themselves. The surrounding world considered them to be Christians, and asked no questions. This, too, won the approval of the *Shulhan Arukh* (Yoreh Deah 157.2), although Maimonides disagreed (*Sefer Mitzvot* Lo Ta-aseh #30).

For Oshry during the Holocaust there was a difference between following a path which had the appearance of permanently abandoning Judaism, like using a baptismal certificate which he prohibited, and on the other hand using a forged Christian passport, a temporary measure, which he permitted. Similarly, he allowed an individual with a non-Jewish name to enter the letters R.K. into a passport, which stood for Roman Catholic in German, to the Nazis, but could be interpreted differently by the Jewish bearer. A parallel decision was given by

Hayim Shor (*Torat Hayim* #17) and Samuel Ungar (*Mekadshei Hashem*, p. 214; R. Kirschner, *Anthology of Holocaust Responsa*, pp. 97 ff). It is clear from these statements that these rabbis took a hard line with a baptismal certificate which seemed like an outright denial of Judaism, but were willing to go along with anything less.

Other authorities during the Holocaust, however, decided differently even on the matter of baptismal certificates. They realized that (a) the Nazis were not interested in converting anyone to Christianity; (b) they made such conversions punishable by death; (c) they severely punished Christian clergy involved in such an act of mercy. For these reasons the number of *Batei Din* in Poland, Czechoslovakia and Hungary, as well as Lithuania, permitted such baptismal certificates to be held by Jews, and treated these Jews as any other member of the Jewish community despite protests within the community. Any other action seemed to play directly in the hands of the Nazis, and the rabbis certainly did not wish to do that (H.J. Zimmels, *The Echo of the Nazi Holocaust in Rabbinic Literature,* pp. 77 ff). Similarly, it was permitted for individuals to declare themselves Karaites as they were not considered Jews under various Nazi rulings (Ibid. 88 ff.).

The main line of thought among both Medieval and modern commentators prohibits an outright denial of Judaism, but permits an ambiguous statement which can be interpreted as a denial by the persecutor. It also permits a disguise which would not cause any questions to be asked.

The Medieval authorities also distinguished types of persecution. If the persecutor wished to force Jews to accept another religion, then it was the duty of the Jew to resist even if it meant death. If, however, it was the intent of the persecutor merely to persecute the Jew and threaten him with death without any interest in turning him into an idol worshipper, then he could simulate idol worship in order to save his life (*Azei Levonah* Yoreh Deah 179; *Turei Zahav* Yoreh Deah 179; *Shulhan Arukh* Yoreh Deah 157.1).

In the period of the Holocaust and the Expulsion from Spain, the identification of Jews and their persecution was a matter of government policy. In 1492, the authorities demanded conversion to Christianity. During the Holocaust everyone of Jewish descent, even Christians, were to be slain. Those conditions were very different from a temporary act of terrorism.

Terrorists usually do not hold their hostages beyond a brief specified period. Furthermore, such terrorists are not interested in bringing about a change in religion, but want to use Jewish hostages for whatever leverage can be exercised through them upon Israel. It is the duty of the remainder of the Jewish community to obtain the freedom of captives whenever this does not endanger the community itself (B. 8b; *Yad* Hil. Matnat Aniyim 8.10; *Shulhan Arukh* Yoreh Deah 252). One great medieval hostage, Meir of Rothenburg, forbade payment of any ransom after he had been taken captive in the thirteenth century as he felt that this would hurt the community and set a bad precedent (Graetz, *Geschichte der Juden* Vol. VII, pp. 173 f; 423 f). In the case of modern hijacking by terrorists potential hostages can help Israel to avoid blackmail and guard themselves from additional danger by hiding their Jewish identity.

It would, therefore, be appropriate for children and adults, if taken hostage by terrorists, to conceal their Jewish identity first through passive acts and then through any other way which is possible.

Walter Jacob

(Walter Jacob, *Contemporary American Reform Responsa*, New York, 1987, # 63).

JEWISH LAWYERS AND TERRORISTS
1989

QUESTION: According to Jewish tradition is a Jewish lawyer obliged to defend Arab terrorists who attempt to kill Jews in Israel if a Jewish lawyer is designated to defend them? Is a Jewish lawyer obliged to defend terrorists who attempt to kill people in general if a Jewish lawyer is designated to defend them? Is a Jewish lawyer obliged to defend a member of the American Nazi Party he knows that the goal of the American Nazi Party is detrimental to Jewish people? (Rabbi Jack Segal, Houston TX)

ANSWER: We should begin by making it clear that the current system of appointing a lawyer or the hiring of a lawyer to defend appears late in our tradition. Although a person might have engaged someone to speak for him, this was usually not an individual who made his livelihood as an attorney. A representative akin to the modern attorney was used if the individual could not appear personally to illness or distance or if one of the parties felt inadequate to the test of presenting a case. Most cases proceeded without an attorney. The traditional Jewish court procedure through the centuries saw judges engaged in interrogation and so they did much of what attorneys do in the American courts. Various responsa mentioned attorneys and dealt with problems associated with them but not with our problem (Jacob ben Judah Weil *Responsa*: Meier of Rothenburg *Responsa;* Isaac ben Sheshet *Responsa* #235; Moses Issserles *Responsa* and others).

Although there is nothing like a court appointed attorney in the traditional system of Jewish law, nevertheless, the tradition may provide some guidance for Jewish attorneys in the United States and in the State of Israel in which the courts function differently. In these systems an accused individual engages an attorney or has an attorney appointed. What is the duty of a Jewish attorney under those circumstances? In order to answer this question, we must ask ourselves about the purpose of a trial. Our *concern* is justice and that was expressed by the Bible which demanded close cross examination of the witnesses (Deut 13.15) as the accused was perceived innocent till proven guilty.

The accused must be present during the examination of each of the witnesses who are testifying against her/him (*Yad* Hil Edut 4.1).

Furthermore, the defendant must be personally warned by those who saw the crime or by someone else (San 30a; Git 33b; Kid 26b and Codes). The examination must concentrate on precise facts and not wander afield (San 32b; *Yad* Hil Edut 18.2; 22:1 ff; *Shulhan Arukh* Hoshen Mishpat 15.3; *Responsa Rivash # 266).* There are strict rules against self incrimination and no evidence of that kind is admissible (Ex 23.1; San 9b; Yeb 25; San 6.2: 18.6 and commentaries). The defendant may plead on her/his own behalf in front of the court before the court begins its deliberations (*M.* San 5:4), but he/she is not permitted to say anything which might prejudice the court against him (San 9:4). If the defendant is not capable of speaking for himself/herself, then a judge may do so for her/him (San 29a). If the matter involves a death sentence, then the court remains in session until the individual has been executed so that if any new evidence appears, the execution may be halted (*M.* San 6.1; San 43a and *Yad* Hil. San. 13.1 (ff.). This is merely a sample of judicial safeguards against injustice; they demonstrate the great care given to the defense of the accused and the efforts made on his behalf by the ancient system of courts. Lawyers or other representatives have not been involved, but the spirit of the law demands that we seek justice. We, in many modern lands, do so through an adversarial procedure.

The spirit of traditional legislation would indicate that lawyers in our system must participate in this effort to seek justice. This would apply to war criminals, terrorists or others who may be tried in the United Sates or in the State of Israel. Jewish attorneys should consider themselves within the framework of tradition if they are appointed to such tasks or wish to volunteer for them. No one can, of course, be forced into such a position against their will. If willing, then they will help to assure that justice is done and that the accused has a reasonable opportunity to defend herself/himself within the framework of our judicial system. "Justice, Justice shall you pursue" (Deut 16.20) or "in righteousness shall you judge your neighbor" (Lev 19.15) will continue to be our guide.

Walter Jacob

(Walter Jacob, *Questions and Reform Jewish Answers – New American Reform Responsa,* New York, 1992 # 238.)

SOLDIER WEARING A SWORD AT A WEDDING
1970

QUESTION: At a recent marriage a military officer was to be married in full dress uniform, which includes the wearing of a sword. Should this be permitted? (From Vigdor W. Kavaler, Pittsburgh, Pennsylvania.)

ANSWER: There has been a wide variety of customs as to what was the proper garment for the groom to wear at his wedding. The Mishnah in *Sotah* IX:14 speaks of the fact that both bride and groom wear a crown, but that this custom in time of persecution was abolished. Maharil, in the fourteenth century in Mainz, describes a wedding in detail and speaks of the groom wearing ashes on his head as a mark of mourning for Jerusalem, and also wearing the *sargenes* (i.e., the *kittel*). In fact it was the custom in Eastern Europe (a custom still followed by many Orthodox people) to consider the wedding day, if not as actually a time of mourning, as at least a time of repentance. This is based upon the Talmudic idea (*j. Bikurim* 65d and Isserles, *Even Ha'ezer* 61:1)that for the bride and groom the wedding day is a day of repentance like the Day of Atonement. Therefore, the bride and groom fast until the wedding ceremony and, therefore, in Eastern Europe (according to some customs) the bride wore a shroud under her wedding gown and the groom wore a *kittel*, the white, shroud-like garment of Yom Kippur. A more general custom, widely observed, was for the groom to wear a *talit*, a custom generally based upon the juxtaposition of the verses in Scripture (Deut. 22:12,13) where the verse: "You shall put fringes upon your garments," comes right before the verse: "If a man takes a women to wife." More romantically explained, the origin of the custom of the groom's wearing a *talit* derives from the fact that the bride makes him a gift of his first *talit* (since unmarried men do not wear the full *talit*), and that the four sets of eight threads in the fringes total thirty-two, which is the numerical equivalent of the Hebrew word *lev*, which means "heart." However, practically speaking, the groom's *talit* was an essential part of the wedding ceremony, since before the development of the *hupah* (wedding canopy) in the late Middle Ages, the custom was (and is still the custom in parts of western Germany) that the groom, during the ceremony, spreads his *talit* over the head of the bride, thus symbolizing their seclusion and their unity. However, most of these customs of special items for the groom and the bride are no longer practiced among some Orthodox Jews, and certainly not among non-Orthodox Jews. Therefore we can say that there is no objection to whatever type of clothes or uniform the bridegroom wears.

Although this, in general, is the case, that in those marriages which are not strictly Orthodox a soldier may be married in his uniform, nevertheless there may be a specific objection to the wearing of a sword, since the sword does seem to symbolize a mood opposite to the mood of unity and love which should prevail at a wedding. Hence the question. Besides this feeling, the very fact that this question was asked is an indication that there is some recollection of some Jewish law that may be directly involved. It is this latter question which concerns us.

The Mishnah in *Berakhot* XI:5 says that it is forbidden to enter the Temple Mount in Jerusalem carrying one's money-belt and one's walking stick. But according to the *Shulhan Arukh* (Orach Chayim 151:6) it is permitted to enter our synagogue (i.e., not the ancient Temple) with staff and money belt. But Joseph Caro adds that "*Some say* that it is forbidden to enter a synagogue with a long knife." In his *Bet Joseph*, his commentary to the *Tur*, he gives the source of this individual opinion. It is taken from the *Orchot Chayim* (Aaron of Lunel) Vol. I, "Laws of the Synagogue," #7, where this prohibition is mentioned in the name of Meir of Rothenburg. The reason given by Meir of Rothenburg as quoted by the *Orchot Chayim* is that the synagogue prolongs life and the "long knife" shortens it.

But this is an individual sentiment, not a law. The *Tur* does not mention it at all. Since it is not a fixed law, we have no right to promulgate it. It is a principle in Jewish law that one may not prohibit that which is permitted.

Moreover, besides its not being a law, when it *is* mentioned it is only with regard to *entering* the synagogue sanctuary. In other words, if the marriage did not take place in the sanctuary itself (say, in the rabbi's study or in a hall) even this individual objection to a "long knife" would not apply.

To sum up: The custom of special garments of mourning to be worn by bride and groom has largely lapsed among most Jews. There is, therefore, no requirements as to the type of garments to be worn. As for the full military officer's uniform which includes a sword, there is only one chance opinion that one should not enter the synagogue with a long knife. But that is not the law and, besides, it applies only to the sanctuary itself.

An analogous question was dealt with recently by Eliezar Waldenberg of Jerusalem in Volume X (#18) of his response series *Tsits Eliezar*. The responsum, of course, reflects the tense situation which prevails at present in Israel. He was answering the question as to whether an Israeli soldier may enter the synagogue with a rifle or a revolver. He calls attention to the fact that the origin of the law prohibiting entering the synagogue with weapons is to be found in *Sanhedrin* 82a (bottom of the page) which cites the text from Numbers 25:7 that Phineas "went forth out of the congregation and took the spear in his hand." From which the Talmud concludes that one may not handle a spear except outside of the congregation or the synagogue.

Waldenberg suggests that it would be better if the bullets were taken out of the rifle or revolver so that while the soldier is in the synagogue these should cease to be lethal weapons. Or he suggests that they may be covered and that, perhaps, the revolver being enclosed in the holster, is not too objectionable. He adds, however, that in time of danger when these men are actively protecting the community, none of the restrictions need apply.

Solomon B. Freehof
(Solomon B. Freehof, *Modern Reform Responsa*, Cincinnati, 1971, # 20).

USE OF "THE LORD'S PRAYER" BY A SOLDIER

QUESTION: We have been asked whether a Jewish soldier may recite the well-known prayer from the Gospel of St. Matthew (Chapter 6) known as "The Lord's Prayer."

ANSWER: Judged merely by its content, this famous prayer has nothing objectionable in it to a Jew, in fact, almost every one of its phrases has been traced to Jewish sources or at least parallels have been found for them in Jewish sources. Nor is the fact that the prayer is of non-Jewish origin sufficient reason to prohibit its use by a Jew. A medieval legend found in a Midrash describes Simon Peter, the first of the Popes, as the author of various *piyyutim* used on the Day of Atonement (see Jellinek, *Bes Ha Midrash*, V, 60 ff; also *Kovetz Ma'asey Ha-gaonim"*, pp. 107–8). The only question involved is whether it is a violation of the law, "Thou shalt not follow their statutes." This law has already been described in a previous responsum and the various limitations of it mentioned. It is only necessary to mention the fact that the law is careful to indicate that not necessarily everything which is customary among Gentiles should be avoided by Jews, but only such that either have no meaning (*Da'as Hevel U'shtus*) or those which are specifically part of their worship. See the explanation of Rabbi Isaac in the famous *Tosfos* to Avoda Zara lla. Joseph Colon (Maharik, Italy, fifteenth century) says clearly, speaking of Christian garments, if a Jewish garment does not express Judaism or modesty any more than the Gentiles wear, then there is no prohibition for the Jews to adopt garments customary among the Gentiles (*Responsa Maharik* #88). This is cited by Joseph Caro in his *Kesev Mishnah* to Maimonides *Yad* Hil. Akum XI,l. and by Isserles to Yore Deah 178 #1. If, however, the custom is generally a part of Gentile worship, then it is prohibited.

A fairly recent, clear statement on this is by Z'vi Dov Eisner in *V'y'laket Joseph*, Vol. IV #88, which he says, the prohibition against following their statutes applies only if the Jew does something which the Gentile does during the time of worshiping his

God. Since "The Lord's Prayer", by its very title refers to the prayer uttered by Jesus, and since it is a definite part of Christian worship, it certainly falls under the prohibition of following the statutes of the Gentiles and should not appropriately be recited by a Jewish soldier.

Of course, a Chaplain when his duty requires of him to conduct non-Jewish worship, is under government command to do so, and that circumstance would fall under a different category.

Solomon B. Freehof , Chairman with Leo Jung, David Aronson
(Responsa to Chaplains 1948–1953, Commission on Jewish Chaplaincy, National Jewish Welfare Board,New York, 1953, # 7).

WEARING A CROSS
1940s

QUESTION: A question was brought to use through a Chaplain with regard to the inquiry of a Jewish nurse as to her wearing a cross with her "dog-tag". The chaplain stated that the question was raised with reference to the possibility of becoming stranded somewhere in the South Pacific area where in many instances the natives had come to recognize the cross as the only sure symbol of friendship.

ANSWER: In the discussion of *Yore Deah* 178:1, where the question is raised about Jews wearing the garments on non-Jews as to when that is prohibited and when permitted, the commentator *Sifte Cohen* says that in times of persecution it is certainly permitted for a Jew to disguise himself by wearing non-Jewish clothes. Thus, if, for example, the question were whether Jewish soldiers fighting on the European continent might not be permitted to conceal their Jewish identity by wearing "dog-tags" without the letter "H" so that, if captured by the Nazis they would not be mistreated, the answer would be that this is certainly permitted.

However, such concealing of Jewish identity cannot be permitted in the South Seas where there is no question of persecution of Jews. The question specifically, however, is not one of concealing Jewish identity, but of wearing the cross in order to win the friendship of natives in the South Seas, who are accustomed to consider the cross as a symbol of friendship. The law on this matter is quite clear. *Shulhan Arukh, Yore Deah* 141:1, Joseph Karo discussing which statues are to be considered idols and which are not, says that the statues in villages are to be considered idols since they are meant to be bowed down to. Those in great cities are not to be considered idols since they are merely for decoration. To this Moses Isserles comments as follows: "A cross which is meant to be bowed down to is forbidden, but one that is worn around the neck is merely a memento and is not forbidden." Thus, the law is clear.

To use a cross as the nurse intended to is not forbidden by law, but since it is clearly against general Jewish sentiment, the Committee refrains from advising her on this matter. She herself must judge how grave the danger is and how much help the symbol would give her.

Solomon B. Freehof, Chairman with Leo Jung and Milton Steinberg
(Responsa in War Time, Division of Religious Activities, National JewishWelfare Board, New York, 1947)

VOLUNTEERING FOR THE MILITARY CHAPLAINCY
1940s

QUESTION: The question has arisen whether it is in accordance with Jewish law to volunteer for the chaplaincy and thus take on the dangers of military life.

ANSWER: There is no question that, in Jewish law, military service, when it is *required* by the government, must be accepted wholeheartedly by subjects or citizens of Jewish faith. The duty to respect the commands of the government is clearly stated and emphasized in Jewish law.   This attitude of respect and loyalty to the government is summarized, for example, in the introductory statement (on page 10) of Isaac Elchanon Spector's *Ein Yitzhak Hasheni* (who quotes Proverbs 24:21, Aboth 3:2, Jer. 29:7, Yoma 69a–Simon the Just to Alexander): The specific duty to serve in the army is described in detail by the Chofetz Chaim (Israel Meir Hacohen of Radun) in his Introduction to *Machanei Yisrael*: "It is a great sin", he says, "to evade service in the army."

This, of course, refers to *compulsory* service which, being the command of the government (tzivui hammemshalo), according to Jewish law must be obeyed.   But our question does not directly concern itself with obeying the command to serve (about which there is no doubt) but volunteering on one's own initiative.   Is such volunteering in accordance with Jewish law?

The basic question involves the laws of *sakkana*, danger to life, as to whether one may put himself in danger and also whether there is not to the contrary the duty to escape from such dangers. There is a definite command in the law to avoid all dangers.   This law has a number of different aspects.   One of them is based upon the verse (Deut. 4:9): "Be careful and preserve your soul."   The Talmud (Berakhot 3a & 8b, et al) speaks of the obligation to guard against endangering oneself by entering a ruin, drinking unsafe water, etc.   Maimonides codifies these various dangers (*Yad*, Hil. Rozeah u-Shemirat Nefesh XI, 4 & 5).   So does the *Tur* and the *Shulhan Arukh* (Yoreh Deah 116).   See especially the long note by Isserles.   Maimonides says that whoever does not avoid such dangers but insists that he takes them at his own risk and that, therefore, it is his own affair, should be flogged for endangering himself (makat mardut).   (So too in *Shulhan Arukh*, Hoshen Mishpat, 427 #9).

In addition to these dangers with regard to which one should avoid exposing himself, there are also the dangers concerning which one should avoid exposing others. These are based upon the command (Deut. 22:8) to put a parapet around the roof of the house. This verse ends with: lo sosim domim b'vesecho," which becomes the key verse in all the later discussions. In the *Sifre* (ad loc.) this law is extended to similar neglect of safeguards, such as leaving a well uncovered, or leaving a stumbling block in the road. This duty to avoid causing danger to oneself and to others is codified in Maimonides (*Yad,* Hil. Rozeach XI, 4) and *Shulhan Arukh*, Hoshen Mishpat 427.

There is a third type of danger due not to carelessness or to neglect as are the above types, but to special circumstances involving the relative safety of a man and his fellowman. Thus, the famous case given in the Talmud (Baba Metziah 62a), of the two men in the desert drinking water enough for only one. Whose life is to be preserved? This is based upon the verse in Leviticus 25:36: "Thy brother shall live with thee," (and is first found in *Sifra* to this verse), and ends with Akiba's statement: "Your life must come first."

Finally, there is the danger involved in the duty of martyrdom. Under which circumstances should one prefer to die rather than commit a sin? This involves the three cardinal sins, the question of whether it is in public or in private, or whether the purpose of the persecutor is to destroy the faith. (Cf. Maimonides, *Yad,* Hil. Yesodei Torah V,1, and *Shulhan Arukh*, Yore Deah 157) Yet even in those cases where it is a duty to accept martyrdom, if he decides to commit the sin and thus avoid the martyrdom, he is considered an "anus" i.e., one who sins not of his own free will, and is to be forgiven. Thus it is clear that in all these four classes of danger, carelessness as to one's food, etc., neglect of precautions such as covering a well, special experiences such as the desert journey, and martyrdom, in all of these it is a general duty to avoid danger.

All the cases mentioned deal with one's personal obligations and, except directly by way of analogy, do not concern the personal danger in fulfillment of one's duty to the government. There is, for example, no direct law which makes use of the verse in Psalm 110,3 which Rashi and Kimchi understand to mean that the people gladly volunteered for war no one was freed from the danger of war but all were obligated to go (M. Sota VIII,7; Maimonides, *Yad*, Hil. Melakhim V, 1-2). All this refers to the wars of Israel. Of course there is, as has been stated, no question as to the duty to obey the command to serve in the armies of the lands of our citizenship, but to what extent is it a moral or religious duty to take on <u>voluntarily</u> the dangers of such war?

As to that there can be no religious mandate, just as there is no secular mandate. Yet David Hoffman in *Melamed L'ho-il*, Orah Hayim 42, in discussing the duty to serve in the army makes clear the fact that it involves *sakana* and *sakana* can lead to violation of the Sabbath; nevertheless he indicates that such violation of the Sabbath involving danger is permitted if the journey or the enterprise is for the purpose of fulfilling a mitzvah, (based chiefly upon *Bet Joseph* to *Tur* Orah Hayim 248). Then he continues that not to serve in the Army involves more than the failure to observe a *mitzvah* but actually a sin of the profanation of the Name because of the effect that such evasion would have on the good name of the Jewish community. With regard to the chaplaincy, both elements are involved. There is certainly the mitzvah of making possible regular worship for the soldiers and also the avoidance of profanation of the Name if too few chaplains would be available. For these two reasons it is permitted to accept Sakana which would lead to violation of the Sabbath. Yet there is a religious duty to keep others from danger and to diminish their peril. He who does not do what he can to save others, violates the command, "Stand not idly by the danger to thy brother" (Lev. 19:16). So Maimonides takes this verse in *Yad*, Hil. Rozeach 1:14. See also Naftali Berlin (Neziv) to *Sheeltot* Exodus 38, who says that one should strive with all his strength to save another up to the risk of his own life.

Does then the work of the chaplaincy tend to strengthen and preserve the life of the soldiers in their time of danger? There is some bearing on this question in the Chofetz Chaim's *Mahanei Yisrael*. In two rather touching chapters (38 and 39) he speaks of the Jewish soldier in the danger of actual battle and dwells upon the duty of prayer and confession and trust in God, assuring his readers that the sincere religious life strengthens the heart and will, in God's goodness, bring protection in time of danger. So, too, we would say that the soldier's spiritual confidence enhances his morale and increases his inner strength and his safety. The chaplain, as he performs his task, fulfills a religious duty. The Gaon Achai said in *Sheeltot* (Exodus #38). It is a high spiritual duty to preserve the body and the spirit.

There is a further question which is dependent upon the one which has been discussed above. The above discussion dealt with whether a man has the right to put *himself* into a place of danger, but there is also the question as to whether one has the right to put others in a place of danger. In other words, the question hitherto has dealt with the Chaplain and his right to volunteer. The second question now deals with the committees of the various organizations and their right to organize the draft or the volunteering.

It should be clear at the outset that it is irrelevant to cite in this discussion the Mishnah in Terumot VIII, 12 (Maimonides *Yad*, Yesodei Torah V, 6 and Isserles in *Shulhan Arukh* Yore Deah 157,1) namely, that if the Akum demand that a Jew be handed over to them for death (or dishonor) that we should not do so (except under special certain circumstances). Meir Eisenstadt (*Imre Eish* Yore Deah #52) shows quite clearly that entering military life is not at all analogous to this demand of persecutors. It is of interest to note that Meir Eisenstadt in the responsum cited above discusses the question of whether it is right for an individual to hire another individual to do his army service for him which was a rather widespread custom in eastern Europe a century ago, and, indeed, was an American custom during the Civil War. In this discussion he deals with all the relevant principles such as handing over a child of Israel to non-Jews, etc., and he decides that such an action (i.e. providing a substitute for oneself) is in no way forbidden by Jewish law.

In general, military life does not involve the question in the Mishnah of being put to death but only the problem of Sakanah. If we would decide that it is wrong for a man to accept this Sakanah, then it would follow that it would be wrong for us to arrange for him to accept it, for then we would be aiding in the committing of a sin. If to volunteer for military service (danger) were a sin, then also the arguments concerning the benefit which such volunteering might bring to the good name of the community would be an insufficient argument. It is a principle in the law that we do not say to a person: Sin thou that we may acquire merit. (Shabbat 42, etc.)

But since, as we have indicated in the discussion above, to accept the danger of military chaplaincy is not a sin, but is to a considerable extent a mitzvah, then our question virtually solves itself. To help in the performance of such a *mitzvah* constitutes a duty on the part of the community and its organizations.

Solomon B. Freehof , Chairman with Leo Jung, David Aronson
(Responsa to Chaplains 1948–1953, Commission on Jewish Chaplaincy, National Jewish Welfare Board, New York, 1953, # 6).

JEWISH TRADITION AND THE CONSCIENTIOUS OBJECTOR
2003

QUESTION: A young Jew who is in the Army Reserve objects to the war on Iraq and wishes to exercise his conscience as a conscientious objector. What is the Jewish attitude toward conscientious objectors; how does the Jewish tradition view this?

ANSWER: Let us view the broader picture regarding the conscientious objector within the Jewish tradition historically. We should note two factors which are relevant to this question. First, the Jewish tradition has little to say on war and military service. As Jews lived in a semi-autonomous condition, virtually a "state within a state," from the fall of the ancient Judean Kingdom in 586 B.C.E. with only a century and a half interruption under the Maccabees and their successors, questions of warfare did not arise. No Jewish philosopher till modern times has dealt with it, nor did the halakhah.

We must ask whether Judaism is opposed to war; is Judaism a pacifist religion or does it contain strains of pacifism? This is a question which deserves a long thorough treatment, however, a brief answer would be negative. Warfare was part of Biblical Israel and was taken for granted. When the prophets spoke about an era of eternal peace and saw it as an ultimate goal, they were speaking of the Messianic Era and expected it to come about through Divine intervention, not human efforts.

Peace was an ultimate hope, but it did not keep the prophets from seeing a divine hand in defeats of Israel and Judah through foreign armies. God used war as punishment for national wrong doing according to their thinking. Nor was warlike imagery foreign to them as they sought to guide the religious and political life of their times.

Now let us turn to an individual claim that his/her conscience is opposed to a particular war. Biblical Judaism with its very few provisions about conscription contains a statement which may appear relevant. When the Israelites formed an army in the Promised Land, they were to be addressed by the officials: "Is there anyone who has built a new house but not dedicated it? Let him go back to the home, let he dies in battle and another dedicate it. Is there anyone who has planted a vineyard but has never harvested it ? Let him go back to his him let he does in battle and another harvest it. Is there anyone who has paid the bride-price for a wife, but who has not yet married her ? Let him go back to his home, let he dies in battle and other marry her." The Official shall go on addressing the troops and say 'Is there anyone afraid and disheartened? Let him o back to his home, lest the courage of his comrades flag like his"(Deut 20:5-8). The later Mishnaic and Talmudic tradition elaborate slightly on these statements, but with no essential changes.

One of its statements deals with the disheartened may provide some guidance - that individual is not afraid, but has some other unknown reasons for not being willing to fight. He is not questioned further, but simply dismissed. To the best of my knowledge no interpretation in the past or the present has included conscientious objectors in this statement. Therefore individuals could be excused from military service for various reasons including fear (Deut 20:5 ff.), but nothing was said about a conscientious objection to a specific war.

Let us, however, also look at the possibility of pacifism within rabbinic Judaism and its view of the jurisdiction of a potential Jewish state. The rabbinic scholars made no statements against warfare and never condemned it outrightly. However, they made the decision to go to war, certainly for *milkhamot reshut* (discretionary war) so difficult that by their standards it would have been impossible. One cannot give this the name of pacifism, but the practical result would have been the same. *Milkhamot reshut* needed the assent of the king, a Sanhedrin (high court consisting of twenty-three), and consultation with the *urim* and *tumim*, i.e. divine permission. As none of these three conditions were possible after the destruction of the Temple and the fall of the last Jewish kingdom, such wars could not be declared.

According to rabbinic Judaism, matters were absolutely different with *milkhamot mitzvah* (mandated war) which meant the conquest and defense of the Land of Israel. There was no halakhic way of being a pacifist when it came to this divinely commanded conquest and defense of the Land of Israel. Those statements are precise and clear.

Now let us view the entire matter in the framework of our lives in a modern secular state to which we have pledged our support. Here the simple statement of *dina demalkhuta dina* (the law of the state is law) guides us. When the question of military service by Jews in the armies of secular states arose in early nineteenth century Europe, this principle was invoked. Jews served in numerous armies including those of lands which oppressed us as Russia. In the lands of western Europe, young Jews volunteered enthusiastically with the hopes of demonstrating their absolute commitment to the modern nation state and receiving complete civil rights. In order to be part of the modern state we have accepted its obligations and laws.

It would be possible to question the entire theory of *dinah demalkhuta dina* and conclude that it does not include endangering one's life for the demands of the state. However, such a selective reading is filled with peril. We know that the state enforces many laws which may endanger human life; it does so in its effort to seek equity and justice for all citizens.

Among modern nation states, only a few have made any provisions for conscientious objectors. The personal conscience was considered irrelevant when national security was at stake. Individuals who refused to do military service were simply punished for evading the law of general conscription. The question was therefore not asked till modern America and some other nations which make provisions for conscientious objectors.

We have looked at this question from a broader point of view. However, the individual involved here is not opposed to war generally as otherwise he would not be part of a military reserve unit. He may in fact have taken part in another war, so the question is whether an individual can object to a particular war. The Jewish tradition would deny that right as well as the general right to object to any and all wars under the rubric *dina demalhutah dina* (the law of the land is the law). The individual may find other grounds for this objection, but there is no basis for them in the Jewish tradition. The laws of the United States permit possible exemption to those who totally object to war and does so on various grounds, but not to selective conscientious objectors.

The stance of this individual has no foundation in Judaism. In a democracy it is possible for him to take a speak out and vote in an attempt to change the path of the nation, but otherwise he is duty-bound to obey the law and serve, even with his mental reservations.

Walter Jacob
(Unpublished responsum)

PACIFISM AND JUDAISM
1989

QUESTION: Is pacifism part of Judaism? Has it been a major factor in Jewish life and thought in the past? Is there a pacifist halakhic tradition within Judaism which we may follow? (Rabbi R. Lehman, New York)

ANSWER: The ideal of peace has been so important in Judaism that we have used it as a common daily greeting –*shalom* with biblical roots for this custom (Gen. 43:23; Ex. 4:18). The biblical prophets emphasized the goal of peace with such statements as: "Peace, peace to him that is far off and to him that is near" (Is. 57:19); "I will make a covenant of peace with them; it shall be an everlasting covenant with them (Ezek. 37:26); "My covenant was with him of life and peace," (Mal. 2:5); "The Lord will bless his people with peace," (Ps 29:11); "seek peace and pursue it (Ps. 34:15); "they shall beat their swords into plowshare and their spears into pruning hooks; nation shall not lift sword against nation, neither shall they learn war anymore," (Micah 4:3; Is 2:4); "the wolf shall dwell with the lamb, the leopard shall lie down with the kid, the calf and the young lion, and the fatling together and a little child shall lead them (Is.11:6).

These statements magnificently proclaimed the Jewish ideal of peace. This was our Messianic dream. The vast rabbinic literature continued to foster it with hundreds of statements; poetry through the ages yearned for it. The halakhah supported it as a noble ideal, but without providing a practical path which would bring it about in the broader world of national strife. The biblical quotations, mentioned above and many others, were mentioned in numerous discussions in an effort to bring about peaceful resolutions in conflict situations through the *bet din*. The goal of justice both in personal conflict and communal strife was attained. Physical violence was curbed and and the bet din rarely invoked physical punishments in its decisions. A peaceful environment was created within the Jewish communities and so the biblical and rabbinic ideal of peace became a reality.

Taking this ideal into the broader world was neither possible nor considered in a theoretical way. No statement forbade war. The halakhic codes make peace on a broader scale their goal and a hold it up as a grand ideal, but do not mandate it.

The *siddur* with its daily public and private prayers constantly pleads with God to bring peace to the entire world. Modern Jews, Reform, Orthodox, or Conservative continue the path of countless generations as we pray to God for world-wide peace and often conclude our services with the biblical blessing "the Lord give you peace" (Nu 6:26).

Modern Jewish thinkers such as Lazarus, Hirsch, Cohen, Baeck, Buber, and Cronbach have stressed the need to work for peace. They sustain this Messianic hope through their writings. A small group of Reform rabbis early in the twentieth century led by Judah Magnes were active pacifists, but their influence soon waned. The goal of permanent peace continued to be fostered by poets and writers in the Jewish communities of Europe, Israel and the North America.

None of this, however led to an ideology of pacifism. Biblical as well as Maccabean and Roman times demonstrate a willingness to fight. As long as a Jewish nation existed, warfare persisted.

When the Jewish leadership understood that further struggles against Rome would not succeed, they channeled national hopes into a Messianic dream, God would eventually bring about a national rebirth. This would occur along with world wide peace.

This was a kind of practical pacifism; it did not prohibit warfare, but left all of this in the hands of God. In the practical personal realm the right of personal self-defense was never questioned, but surrounded by halakhic restrictions. Personal and communal conflicts were settled through the *bet din*. Justice on this practical level brought peace.

Military service was not questioned in the Bible or the post-biblical literature as the Books of Maccabees clearly demonstrated. The defeat by the Romans in 70 C.E. and again after the revolt of Bar Kochba in 134 C.E. brought the realization that further combat had to be avoided. The dream of a self-governing state was changed to be Messianic The midrashic and talmudic literature minimized tales of conflict and heroism. The festival of Hannukah and centered around a minor miracle rather than military achievement. At the same time, the biblical military heroes were changed into literary or poetic figures. For the next two thousand years Jews occasionally fought on the walls of medieval cities along with their neighbors, but only in extreme emergencies. The soldier was not glorified.

The question of regular military service never arose. Jews formed a separate community wherever we lived till the Emancipation at the beginning of the nineteenth century. Only Emancipation, the slow movement toward citizenship, and the modern state's hunger for manpower to feed its national armies conscripted Jews into military service. At first we entered unwillingly, but then, caught up in the fervor of nationalism, volunteered in large numbers.

This eagerness to serve, first shown throughout nineteenth century western Europe, was the clearest demonstration that whatever impulse toward pacifism, beyond the personal and communal, may have existed, had never taken root. We abandoned warfare after endless Roman defeats. Had we fought, we would have been wiped out. We were pacifists for almost two millennia, but never claimed this as a willing heritage. A longing for peace always remained, but hoping for the goal of peace and even praying for it are very different from pacifism which demands a thorough going ideology..

It is bizarre that Jews, who were what we might well call unwilling pacifists – forced into that situation by the surrounding world – never developed an ideology of pacifism. Pacifism has not become central to any major Jewish thinker. We took the ideal and furthered it personally and within the community. However, we left it as a an ideal, possibly a Messianic dream.

Perhaps it is the realism of Judaism which recognized that such a stance on a broader level would only lead to annihilation. The rest of the world might even admire it, but would not emulate it. We long for world-wide peace, further it in every way possible, but recognize that conditions in the world are still far from it.

Walter Jacob
(unpublished responsum)

CONTRIBUTORS

Solomon B. Freehof (1893–1990) was rabbi of the Rodef Shalom Congregation, Pittsburgh, Pennsylvania; past President of the Central Conference of American Rabbis, and the World Union for Progressive Judaism; past Chair of the Responsa Committee, Central Conference of American Rabbis; author of twenty-six books including eight volumes of responsa, *Stormers of Heaven* (1931), *Modern Jewish Preaching* (1941), *Preface to Scripture (1950), Reform Jewish Practice* (1947, 1952), The *Responsa Literature* (1955), *The Book of Job* (1958), *A Treasury of Responsa* (1963), *New Reform Responsa* (1980), *Today's Reform Responsa* (1990).

Walter Jacob is President of the Abraham Geiger College in Berlin/Potsdam; Senior Scholar of Rodef Shalom Congregation, Pittsburgh, Pennsylvania; President of the Freehof Institute of Progressive *Halakhah* and the Associated American Jewish Museums. Author, editor, or translator of thirty-nine books including *Christianity through Jewish Eyes* (1974), *American Reform Responsa* (1983), *Contemporary American Reform Responsa (1987), Liberal Judaism and Halakhah* (1988), *The Second Book of the Bible: Exodus Interpreted by Benno Jacob* (1992), *Die Exegese hat das erste Wort* (2002), *The Environment in Jewish Law (2003), Pursuing Peace Across the Alleghenies* (2005), *Hesed and Tzedakah - From the Bible to Modernity (2006), Only in America - The Open Society and Jewish Law* (2009).

Michael Stroh is the Executive Director of the Toronto Board of Rabbis, Rabbi Emeritus of Temple Har Zion in Thornhill, Ontario, past-president of Arzenu: International Federation of Reform and Progressive Religious Zionists and ARZA Canada. He has taught at the Hebrew Union College–Jewish Institute of Religion, the University of Waterloo, St. Michael's College of the University of Toronto. He has written extensively on Reform Judaism.

Mark Washofsky is the Solomon B. Freehof Professor of Jewish Law, Hebrew Union College–Jewish Institute of Religion in Cincinnati, Ohio. Chair of the Responsa Committee of the Central Conference of American Rabbis. He has published numerous studies in the field of Jewish law, legal theory and contemporary ethics. He is the editor of *Teshuvot for the Nineties* (1997), and author of *A Guide to Jewish Living and Practice* (2000).

Arnold Jacob Wolf (1924–2008) was rabbi, K.A.M. Isaiah Israel Congregation, Chicago. A major figure in civil rights as well as international peace efforts; he was the founder and leader of *Breira*, an organization for peace in the Middle East.He has published over two hundred articles. Among his books are *Rediscovering Judaism* (1965),*Unfinished Rabbi* (1998), *Broken Tablets* (1999) He taught at HUC–JIR in New York, at Yale University and Spertus College in Chicago.

Moshe Zemer is Director of the Freehof Institute of Progressive *Halakhah* in Israel,a founder of Progressive Judaism in Israel and founding rabbi of the Kedem Synagogue-Bet Daniel, Tel Aviv. He is *Av Bet Din* of the Israel Council of Progressive Rabbis and Senior Lecturer in rabbinics at Hebrew Union College, Jerusalem. He has contributed many articles on *halakhah* to the Israeli press. He is author of *The Sane Halakhah* (1993).